The Secret History of
ENGLISH SPAS

The Secret History of
ENGLISH SPAS

MELANIE KING

BODLEIAN
LIBRARY
PUBLISHING

*Dedicated to my very special friends Josephine, Elaine, Hazel
and not forgetting Sue, who passed away in February 2020*

First published in 2021 by the Bodleian Library
Broad Street, Oxford OX1 3BG
www.bodleianshop.co.uk

ISBN 978 1 85124 453 9

Publisher: Samuel Fanous
Managing Editor: Deborah Susman
Editor: Janet Phillips
Picture Editor: Leanda Shrimpton
Production Editor: Susie Foster
Cover design by Dot Little at the Bodleian Library
Text designed and typeset by Lucy Morton of illuminati in 12 on 16 Perpetua
Printed and bound in China by C&C Offset Printing Co. Ltd
on 140 gsm Chinese Golden Sun woodfree paper

British Library Catalogue in Publishing Data
A CIP record of this publication is available from the British Library

ENDPAPERS *Panoramic View of Buxton*, nineteenth-century engraving by Newman & Co., published by John Cumming Bates.
OVERLEAF Map from John Feltham, *Guide to Watering Places*, 1803–06.

CONTENTS

SCO...

IRELAND

Newton Stewart
Stranrawer
Glenluce
Wigton
Fo...
Carrickfergus
Port Patrick
Donaghadee
Mull of Galloway
Belfast
Downpatrick
Dundalk
Droghada

I R I S H   S E...

I. of Man

Droghada
Dublin
Holy Head
I. of Anglesey
Bangar...
Newburgh
Beau...
Caarnarvon
Wicklow
Newin
Llanrust
Harlei...
Arklow
Dolgel...
Cardigan Bay
Dinas...
ABERYSTWITH
Lla...
Wexford
Ne...
Llanarth
Llanbader
Cardigan
Newport
Buil...
St. Davids
Fiskard
Llanymdovry
St. Brides B.
Haverford West
Caarmarthen
Tavern Spite
Bi...
Milford Hav.
TENBY
Blandilhy
Abery...
Pembroke
Neath
Cia...
Caldy I.
SWANSEA
Landgo...

ST GEORGE'S CHANNEL

B R I S T O L   C H A N N E L

Lundy I.
ILFRACOMB
Minehed
Hunts...
Hartland
Biden...
Barnstaple
Stratton
Torrington
Dulverton
Padstow
Camelford
Tiverton
Taunton
St. Columb
Launceston
Okehampton
Arminster
St. Michael
Bodmin
Tavistock
Exeter
St. Ives
Truro
Fowey
Lostwithiel
Tepsham
SIDMOU...
St. Ja...
St. Agnes
Helston
St. Maes
Plymouth
Iw Br
DAWLISH
Lafont...
Penzance
Falmouth
Totness
Newton
TEIGNMOUTH
SHALDON
Dartmouth
Modbury
Lizard Pt.
Dodbrook
Start Pt.

E N G L ...   I S...

The
Great Roads
of
ENGLAND & WALES
connecting the
Watering Places

Scale of Miles.
10   20   30   40   50

GERMAN OCEAN

C H A N N E L

Selected place names as labelled on the map:

Coldstream, Kelso, Berwick, Holy I., Jedburgh, Castleton, Whittingham, Annan, Longtown, Alnwick, Bellingham, Morpeth, Holm, Carlisle, Glaawhett, Tinmouth, Wigton, Hexham, Newcastle, Penrith, Sunderland, Keswick, Appleby, Durham, Hartlepool, Hawkshead, Bowes, Bernard Castle, Stockton, Cartmel, Kendal, Richmond, Hartlepool, Burton, Askrig, Catterick, Guisbrough, Whitby, Horby, N. Allerton, Helmesley, SCARBOROUGH, Lancaster, Settle, Rippon, Thirsk, Flamborough, Poulton, Gisborn, Skipton, Boroughbr., Malton, Preston, Knightly, Otley, Ripley, HARROWGATE, Beverley, Hornsey, Wigan, Halifax, Leeds, York, Tadcaster, Hull, Patrington, Liverpool, Wakefield, Ferrybridge, Weighton, Spurn Hd, Manchester, Barnesley, Doncaster, Barton, R. Humber, Warrington, Stockport, Rotheram, Gainsborough, Grimsby, Knutsford, Disley, Sheffield, Bawtry, Saltflet, Chester, BUXTON, Chesterfield, Retford, Market Raisin, Newcastle, MATLOCK, Mansfield, Tuxford, Lincoln, church, Darlaston, Ashborn, Newark, Shrewsbury, Stafford, Derby, Nottingham, Sleaford, Newport, Burton, Boston, The Wash, Burnham Wells, Montgomery, Lichfield, Loughborough, Wrantham, Bourn, Walsingham, CROMER, Bridgenorth, Wolverhampton, Meriden, Okeham, Uswerth, Potting, Lynn, Ludlow, Birmingham, Leicester, Stamford, Wisbeach, Norwich, Broomsgrove, Coventry, Harborough, Peterborough, Swanham, Watton, YARMOUTH, Worcester, Warwick, Daventry, Kettering, Oundle, Chatteris, Brandon, Beccles, Stratford, Wellingford, Stilton, Ely, Thetford, Loestoff, MALVERN, Camden, Northampton, St. Neots, Huntingdon, Bury, Saxmundham, Tewkesbury, Stratford, Bedford, Cambridge, St. Edmunds, Stow, Aldborough, Dean, CHELTENHAM, Banbury, Buckingham, Eaton, Newmarket, Ipswich, Alcester, Morton, Throp, Aylesbury, Royston, Sudbury, Harwich, Cirencester, Burford, Oxford, Dunstable, Welwyn, Colchester, Farringdon, Wheatly, Watford, St. Albans, Ware, Dunmow, Maldon, Chippenham, Wallingford, Uxbridge, Barnet, Epping, Chelmsford, Rayleigh, Marlborough, Maidenhead, London, Romford, SOUTH END, Devizes, Hungerford, Reading, Hounslow, Thames, Warminster, Newbury, Bagshot, Orpington, Gravesend, MARGATE, Amesbury, Andover, Basingstoke, Guildford, Ryegate, Feversham, Rochester, BROADSTAIRS, Stockbridge, Alton, Farnham, Dorking, Sevenoaks, Maidstone, Canterbury, RAMSGATE, Salisbury, Ramsey, Winchester, TUNBRIDGE, Ashford, Dover, Sandwich, SOUTHAMPTON, Petersfield, Horsham, E. Grinstead, Cranbrook, Deal, Grimbrook, Hithe, Folkstone, LYMINGTON, Midhurst, Chichester, Cuckfield, Lewes, Rye, Hithe, Romney, Dover, Pool, Grimbrook, Arundel, Shoreham, Newhaven, Winchelsea, Straits of Dover, Ostend, Cowes, Newport, I. of Wight, Portsmouth, BOGNOR, WORTHING, BRIGHTHELMSTONE, EASTBOURNE, HASTINGS, Gravelines, Calais, LITTLEHAMPTON, Boulogne

ONE

Salus per Aquam

THE ORIGINS OF ENGLISH SPAS

Spas conjure up images of luxurious pampering: a young couple splashing around in a heated, bubbling jacuzzi, each sipping from a champagne flute. Their dressing gowns, white and fluffy, are draped over lounge chairs, and piped music, setting the mood of sumptuous bliss, mingles with the sound of gurgling water. Bamboo massages are on offer, as are waxes, pedicures, detox therapies, aqua aerobics, body masks, ocean wraps, deep tissue massages and dry flotation treatments.

It all seems a very twenty-first-century phenomenon. Indeed, with wellness and stress relief an increasing priority for holiday-makers in search of relaxation, the spa industry (at least before the pandemic) has been booming: the UK has some 800 residential and hotel spas, while in 2014 the United States boasted more than 20,000, double the number around only a decade earlier.[1] Yet visiting a spa, either to undergo a medical cure or to be luxuriously pampered, is certainly not a new or even modern phenomenon. People in Britain have been 'taking the waters' for many centuries. Mineral waters were both drunk and bathed in, and the waters were warm, hot or cold, and contained hydrogen sulphide, salts or iron, and other minerals. Seventeenth- and eighteenth-century Britain

Two women bathe in the *frigidarium* in an imagined scene at the baths in Pompeii. Sir Lawrence Alma-Tadema, *A Favourite Custom,* oil on wood, 1909.

could boast almost as many spas as we have today. A 1760 treatise gave eighty-seven places around Britain (by no means a comprehensive list) in which to take the waters for the sake of various illnesses. Waters from Malton Spaw in the North Riding of Yorkshire treated ulcers and scabs, while three pints a day from the St Erasmus Well in Staffordshire cured a woman with 'a loathsome Scurf all over her Body'. Water from a well at the Dog and Duck, a public house in Lambeth, could be used for everything from pimples to breast cancer and leprosy, and that from Astrop Wells in Northamptonshire 'restores a Constitution weakened by hard drinking'; these same waters were supposedly effective for 'some sorts of Madness and Melancholy'. Meanwhile, water from Shapmore in Westmorland ended the agony of one sufferer's fourteen-year martyrdom to piles.[2]

The visitors to these baths and wells were legion. Many prominent figures were among them. Numerous kings and queens took the waters, but spas also welcomed a varied group of luminaries: Oliver Cromwell (Wellingborough), Samuel Pepys (Barnet Physic Well), Josiah Wedgwood (Bath), George Frederick Handel (Scarborough), Fanny Burney (Bath), Elizabeth Montagu (Tunbridge Wells), Lord Byron (Matlock), Jane Austen (Bath), Charles Darwin (Malvern and Ilkley) and Charles Dickens (Beulah Spa in Croydon). Many of the mineral wells are long gone. Beulah Spa closed in the 1850s; the only traces that remain are a memorial stone and the name of a local street, Spa Hill. Indeed, the presence of Britain's wells and spas are inscribed in many streets and place names around the country – Coldwell Street, Coldbath Square, Hotwell Road, Holywell Lane, Well Walk, Camberwell, Clerkenwell, Bath, Bath Row, Tunbridge Wells, Leamington Spa, to name only a few.

The wells and spas of Britain were popular places of recreation as well as of treatment and recuperation. The medicinal benefits of bubbling springs were far from the only reason to visit spa towns such as Tunbridge Wells, Epsom, Buxton or Matlock in the seventeenth or eighteenth centuries. Just as today's spa-goers enjoy underwater music and raw food cafés, so too did visitors in previous centuries experience various social and cultural delights: theatrical performances, musical concerts, bowling greens, dances in ballrooms and gaming in casinos. There was also gossip to be enjoyed, and even the possibilities of illicit sexual encounters, marriage matches and political intrigues. Visiting an English spa during this period was a unique experience, and spas would help to shape the etiquette and cultural values of English society.

WHAT HAVE THE ROMANS EVER DONE FOR US?

'Public baths!' shouts an activist in Monty Python's *Life of Brian* (1979) when John Cleese's character, plotting revolution, asks what the Romans have done for them. He had a point. We can thank the Romans for making bathing a far more complex and entertaining ritual than mere immersion in water to cleanse the grubby body. However, communal baths in Britain pre-existed the Romans. New evidence unearthed by researchers at the University of Reading suggests that some Britons were luxuriating in baths before the Romans arrived in 43 CE, since at Silchester in Hampshire archaeologists have discovered an ancient bathhouse beneath the Roman one.[3]

Roman bathhouses, both on the Continent and in ancient Britannia, offered other comforts and amenities to their patrons: libraries, reading rooms, booths selling food and perfume, theatrical and musical performances, and areas for athletic competitions and exercise. The local baths, not expensive to use, were utilized not only for personal hygiene but also as gathering areas for people to relax and keep up with the latest news.

There were as many as a thousand public baths in Ancient Rome. The Baths of Caracalla, one of the largest and most impressive of the city's ancient ruins, reveals the Romans' commitment to bathing. Bathing was a complicated and multi-step ritual, consisting of much more than simply plunging into a tub of water and scrubbing behind the ears. Typically, a visitor would strip off and exercise in *palaestra*, which included a gymnasium. The Ancient Romans must have pumped iron, since Seneca the Younger (*c.* 4 BCE–65 CE), who lived above a public bath, claimed that he could hear the grunting of men 'flourishing leaden weights'.[4] Once a sweat was worked up, the visitor would bathe in the *tepidarium* (warm bath), which prepared him for the *caldarium*, a hot sauna. Masseurs would be on hand to rub scented oils into the skin to rid the body of impurities before the patron returned to the *tepidarium* and then, to cool down, to the *frigidarium* (cold bath). Only after completing this circuit would he head for the *natatio* (swimming pool) to swim or else to socialize. In the Baths of Caracalla the *natatio* was 54 metres long by 23 metres wide – larger than an Olympic-size swimming pool.

A Roman bath complex required incredible engineering skills, which included a system that heated and supplied hot water to the pools. They were also places of great beauty, their floors elegantly tiled with mosaics, their walls decorated with frescoes, and water fountains strategically placed. The Baths of Caracalla featured some of the most impressive statuary in all of Rome, including the 10-foot-high marble statue now known as the Farnese Hercules.

However, Seneca's complaints about the behaviour of the people in public baths takes a bit of the gloss off this appealing picture of expensive marble-and-fresco elegance. He was disturbed not only by the grunting and panting of the weightlifters, but also by the slapping sounds of people getting a 'cheap rubdown' or leaping into the pool, by the commotion caused by the arrest of 'an occasional roisterer or pickpocket', and by 'the hair-plucker with his penetrating, shrill voice … continually giving it vent and never holding

'Tepidarium at Baths of Caracalla'. Illustration from *Wonders of the Past: The Romance of Antiquity and Its Splendours*, ed. J.A. Hammerton, 1923–4. A *tepidarium* is a warm bath.

View of the Roman baths at Bath, constructed in around 70 CE

his tongue except when he is plucking the armpits and making his victim yell instead'. He was also irritated by the cries of people selling cakes and sausages in the bathhouse.[5]

As the Romans conquered Europe they took advantage of the natural hot springs they encountered at places such as present-day Aix-les-Bains and Vichy in France, Aachen and Wiesbaden in Germany, Baden in Austria, and Budapest in Hungary. When the Romans discovered the only two naturally hot thermal waters in England – those in Bath (which they called Aquae Sulis) and Buxton (Aquae Arnemetiae) – they too were developed to Roman standards, with reservoirs built to control the flow of water.

The Romans dedicated the source of the Bath springs to Minerva, the goddess of wisdom, and built a temple around it in about 60 CE. Over the next three hundred years the hot water supplied the bathing complex that allowed Romans and Britons to swim in the waters: over 1 million litres of it, containing forty-two minerals, still flow into Bath each day, at a temperature of 45°C (113° F).

It was not, however, the Romans who first discovered Bath's hot springs but rather, so legend has it, a drove of pigs belonging to Bladud, son of the King of the Britons. Centuries before the Romans arrived in the British Isles, young Bladud contracted leprosy during his studies in Athens. Realizing he would never inherit the throne with this unfortunate condition, Bladud became an outcast on his return home. He found work as a lowly swineherd, but his pigs contracted the disease as he drove them along the Avon valley. They were miraculously cured after rolling in the hot mud around a sulphurous hot spring. Following their lead, Bladud jumped into the mud and he, too, was cured. He returned home, eventually inherited the throne from his father, and dedicated the springs to Sulis,

The legendary King Bladud as depicted in John Wood the Elder's *Essay towards a Description of Bath*, 1765.

the goddess of healing. However, the legend does not exactly end well for Bladud, one of history's first 'birdmen'. Trying to fly with the help of a pair of feathered wings, he flung himself into the air and broke his neck in the fall.[6]

HOLY WATERS

As the Roman Empire declined, so too did the thermal baths of Aquae Sulis and Aquae Arnemetiae. The buildings fell into disrepair or were destroyed, and only the poor tended to use them. The French historian Jules Michelet famously described the centuries after the fall of the Roman Empire as 'a thousand years without a bath'.[7]

Michelet was exaggerating, but in the fifth century the Church declared that warm baths were sinful. Pope Gregory the Great (r. 590–604) stressed that baths were 'for the needs of the body ... not for the titillation of the mind and sensuous pleasure'.[8] Or, as St Jerome proclaimed: 'He that is once washed in Christ needs not to wash again.' Indeed, in the Eastern Church the concept of *alousia*, or abstinence from washing, had been born as a form of asceticism. Cleanliness, for the early Church, was not necessarily next to godliness. Purity of the soul was of much greater value than cleanliness of the body, as Pope Leo I (r. 440–461) stressed in the inscription he had placed over the fountain in St Paul Outside the Walls in Rome: 'Water removes dirt from the body, but faith, purer than any spring, cleanses sin and washes souls.' The Rule of St Augustine stated that bathing was to be done for purposes of health alone. Most convents and abbeys possessed bath facilities, but these were for effecting cures rather than rinsing away the dirt and grime. In Benedictine abbeys, bathing was reserved for the sick, the very young, the very old and guests.

While ancient physicians such as Galen and Celsus had extolled the curative powers of bathing, many doctors in the Middle Ages believed that, on the contrary, hot baths upset the humours. The Jewish philosopher Maimonides (1135–1204), following the Romans, allowed that bathing could have a therapeutic value, but he recommended that one should not bathe more than once every ten days. 'Physicians have noted that frequenting the bath every day corrupts the humours', he wrote, adding pointedly: 'This statement is true.'[9] Even worse, bathing was believed to spread the plague and other diseases. Bathing had been practised sporadically in Western Europe until 1348, when public baths were blamed for spreading the Black Death. According to the famous French physician Ambroise Paré, steam baths opened the pores, allowing 'pestiferous vapour' of the plague to enter the body.[10] Bathing became the activity of the 'uncivilized'. The stigma lasted for many centuries, since a Victorian advocate for bathing complained that his countrymen believed bathing was the habit of 'the wild Irish, the Red Indian, the cruel Turk, or the enslaved Russian'.[11] Baths also had another connotation, with the public ones in Southwark (known as 'stews' after the Old French estuver, 'to bathe') so notorious for prostitution and other illicit sexual activity that Henry VIII shut them down in 1546.

If its moral and medicinal qualities were both suspect, water was believed to possess, by the Middle Ages, a healing spiritual power. Besides the warm waters of Bath and Buxton, the British Isles featured many cold-water springs to whose waters miraculous curative properties were soon attributed. These sites were tolerated by the Church because they were dedicated to saints and known as 'holy wells', and because their waters were drunk (or sometimes applied topically) rather than used for bathing. In an era when physicians and surgeons were almost as dangerous as the diseases they claimed to treat, visiting these wells for healing made an attractive option for someone suffering illness.

Approximately 450 of these holy wells existed in Britain, and many provided, for a fee, both chapels and resident priests as part of the healing package. Drinking the waters for medicinal purposes was performed to the accompaniment of prayers and offerings. Different wells specialized in particular ailments. For example, St Winifred's Well in Flintshire was reputed to cure St Anthony's fire (the skin disease known as erysipelas), St Magnus Well in Yorkshire treated afflictions of the eyes, while St Anne's Well in Buxton was dedicated to disabled people (St Anne was the patron saint of the lame). Another well used by disabled people was Camberwell in London, whose name means 'well of the crippled'.

DISSOLUTION OF THE WELLS

Henry VIII did not merely shut down the stewhouses of Southwark. The tradition of visiting a holy well for medicinal purposes began to decline during the Reformation. Henry had visited the holy well at Binsey, near Oxford, with his first wife, Catherine of Aragon, in hopes of producing a male heir. Following his break with Pope Clement VII, however, Henry came to regard well-worship as a superstitious practice linked to Roman Catholicism. More particularly, he also feared the wells were being used as meeting places for those rejecting the Protestant faith and clinging to Catholicism. In 1536 he ordered one of his courtiers, Sir William Bassett, to destroy St Anne's Well in Buxton and St Mudwell in Burton-on-Trent. Sir William proved a faithful servant, reporting back that, in order to stamp out idolatry and superstition, 'I did not only deface the tabernacles and places where they did stand, but also did take away crutches, shirts, and sheets, with wax offered, being things that did allure and entice the ignorant people to the said offering.'[12]

Other wells were to suffer the same fate. Yet, however linked they had been to religion, the wells also satisfied a communal need since they continued to be used as focal points for social gatherings during the summer months. One such festival the ecclesiastical authorities tried to ban was well-dressing, a custom which originated with the Celts, who placed local flowers and shrubbery on wells to thank the water spirits. Well-dressing waned until the Christians adapted it for their own purposes, with villagers in Tissington, in Derbyshire, among the first to reintroduce the tradition. After surviving the Black Death in the middle of the fourteenth century, the villagers gave thanks not to the water spirits but, rather, to God. Tissington's remoteness allowed the custom to continue even as the Reformation took hold. As this revamped version of well-dressing spread in the north of England, the clergy became integral to the ritual.

Centuries later, well-dressing would be incorporated into a public holiday when, during the Industrial Revolution, Wakes Week,[13] an unpaid holiday in the north of England and the Midlands, was forced upon workers when collieries, mills and factories needed to close for annual maintenance. Although paid holidays have replaced Wakes Week, well-dressing continues as a popular annual event, having become a huge tourist attraction throughout the Peak District from May to September. Designs are planned a year in advance with village committees voting on themes and materials applied. In 2009, Tissington, with a

Tissington Well Dressing, Derbyshire, 2017.

population of only 150, attracted over 50,000 visitors to admire its dressings. The local clergy lead a procession around the village to bless the wells, but many of the designs today are secular, representing topical themes of the day.

Henry VIII and the reformers might have sealed most of the wells and destroyed the Catholic shrines, but many people still sought out the waters for healing. Buxton evidently enjoyed a revival following the depredations of Sir William Bassett. It was one of seven wells

reopened by Queen Elizabeth I after she came to the throne in 1558. When she gave her cousin, rival and prisoner Mary Stuart – Mary, Queen of Scots – permission to visit in the 1570s, Buxton's well was fully functional as a place of leisure: it boasted a bathhouse that doubled as a thirty-room hotel, endless pints of mineral water (several of which were to be consumed each day), games of bowls and archery, 'and other necessaries most decent'.[14] These casual pursuits – another of which included a game for women called

Spa in Belgium, popular for its spring water since the fourteenth century. From a 1647 woodcut in Mathias Merian's *Topographia Westphaliae*.

'troule in Madame' – reveal Elizabeth's attempts to detach the holy
wells from their spiritual origins, and to turn them into social and
medicinal sites rather than religious ones, complete with recreations
and leisure pursuits. Indeed, Mary became so fond of Buxton that
when staying at the New Hall (now the Old Hall Hotel) to enjoy
the town's waters, she supposedly used her diamond ring to scratch
a message on her bedroom window frame: 'Buxton whose fame
thy milk warm waters tell / Whom I perhaps shall see no more,
Farewell.'[15]

SPAS AND SPIES

The 25-year-old Queen Elizabeth had been little troubled by English
Catholics upon her accession. However, within a decade the political
situation changed with the arrival in England of Mary, Queen of
Scots, in 1568, the Rising of the North a year later (when Catholic
nobles from the north of England hoped to depose her in favour of
Mary), and finally the excommunication of Elizabeth by Pope Pius
V in 1570. The New Hall in Buxton, so favoured by Mary, became
such a centre of traitorous plots against the crown that it was named
'the house of Royal intrigue'.

Elizabeth was aware that many Catholics crossed the Channel on
the pretext of taking the waters at places such as Spa in the Spanish
Netherlands. The name 'Spa' originates from the Roman phrase
Salus per Aquam, 'health through water'. Some 20 miles south-east
of Liège, in present-day Belgium, Spa has been a place of healing
since the fourteenth century, when an ironmonger was cured by
drinking the waters from a nearby spring. The small resort quickly
became a gathering place of English Catholic exiles and malcontents.
Here, beyond the reach of English law, they hatched plots against
Elizabeth. One of those resident in Spa in the 1570s – following his
involvement in the Rising of the North – was Henry Parker, the
eleventh Baron Morley, described to King Philip of Spain as 'one

of the best and most Catholic gentlemen of this kingdom and much attached to your Majesty's service'.[16] Another visitor, who came to be cured of urine retention in 1585, was William Allen, an English cardinal who was attempting to commit both the Pope and the king of Spain to the 'enterprise of England' — that is, its invasion and conversion. Among his possessions were such 'explosive matters of high espionage' that, as his condition worsened, he burned everything.[17]

Elizabeth sent spies to follow them. Meanwhile, to deter such foreign travel to Catholic lands, she allowed the transformation of the holy wells into 'spaws', a name meant to connote the same healing properties of Spa, albeit in a domestic and secularized setting. Elizabeth allowed wells to operate so long as the curative properties were claimed to be based on the special properties of the waters themselves rather than, as in times past, on miraculous intervention. The curative powers of the English wells was thus transferred from the Catholic saints to the chemical composition of the waters. The religious faith inherent in well-worship was about to be swept away by scientific and medical studies.

TWO

Taking the Plunge

THE DEVELOPMENT OF SPAWS IN ENGLAND

The first great advocate in England for bathing was Dr William Turner, an anti-Catholic polemicist who had been exiled under Queen Mary. In 1562 he published a treatise in favour of mineral waters: *A Book of the Natures and Properties as well of the Baths in England as of other Baths in Germany and Italy*. Turner was well educated and well travelled, having studied medicine at Cambridge before departing for further studies on the Continent. He received his medical qualifications at the university in Bologna, followed by an Oxford medical degree when he returned to England. A man of many talents and interests, he became a noted botanist and ornithologist, publishing works such as *Names of Herbes* and *Turner on Birds*.

When he turned his attention to bathing, Dr Turner departed sharply from the prevailing view that bathing was bad for the health. However, he suggested certain precautions, offering helpful advice as to how one should bathe. His particular emphasis was on hygiene. He recommended keeping bathers away from where the spring rose, so as not to contaminate the waters; drilling a hole in the bottom of each bath for daily emptying and cleaning; and venting the roof of bathhouses in order to allow the vapours to escape. He frowned

PREVIOUS PAGES *The Baths at Louèche*, detail, by Hans Bock the Elder, 1597.

on mixed bathing (moral hygiene was important) and recommended separate bathing for the sick. He also believed that horses could benefit from mineral baths, advocating the application of leeches to horses standing in waters up to their bellies. Turner lamented what he called the ruinous condition of English baths. He called for their upkeep because of the innumerable health benefits to be derived from them. The waters of Bath alone, he claimed, could treat sixty conditions: a full gamut running from infertility, rheumatism, gout and skin diseases, to intestinal worms and forgetfulness.

A decade later, a Welshman, Dr John Jones, likewise promoted the benefits of mineral waters. Like Turner, he took a thoroughly scientific approach. The full title gives the flavour of his secular evangelizing: *The bathes of Bathes ayde: wonderfull and most excellent agaynst very many sicknesses, approved by authoritie, confirmed by reason, and dayly tryed by experience, with the antiquitie, commoditie, property, knowledge, use, aphorismes, diet, medicine, and other thinges to be considered and observed.* Dr Jones appealed to reason and experience. That same year he published a treatise on the 'auncient Bathes of Buckstones', or Buxton. Many more treatises would follow, likewise extolling and legitimizing – through the language of natural science – the natural health benefits of visiting local baths and spas. All of them prepared a public for the healing benefits of drinking what was often a murky, rust-coloured, bad-tasting water, or bathing with other invalids amid sulphurous fumes in tepid, malodorous waters.

One of the converts appears to have been William Shakespeare, who believed, theoretically at least, in the healing powers of warm baths. In one of his sonnets he writes of water flowing from a spring and into 'a seething bath which yet men prove / Against strange maladies a sovereign cure' (Sonnet 153).[1] In another sonnet he writes of a warm bath as a 'healthful remedy / For men diseased' (Sonnet 154).[2] Diseased men and women would soon be seeking healthful remedies in all corners of the kingdom.

Dr John Jones in his 1572 treatise had extolled the water of Bath as 'amonge all the most marualouse workes of nature'. He claimed that there was nothing more excellent for 'the helpe of the disseased, and amendement of the enfeebled partes of man'.[3] However, Bath in the 1570s was little prepared to exploit these miraculous waters. About a hundred miles west of London, it was a small town of

A detail of Bath, from a larger map of Somerset by John Speed, 1611.

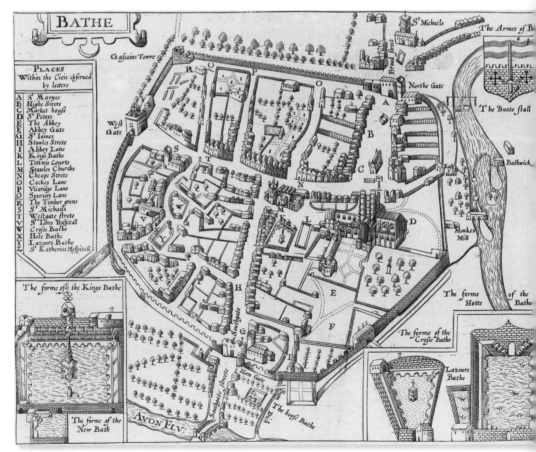

some 300 houses and little more than a thousand people, along with eleven inns and various lodging houses scattered through its narrow streets. The ancient baths were in a state of decay, consisting of little more than pools of water surrounded by seats.

In the summer of 1574, two years after Dr Jones published his treatise, Queen Elizabeth and her court paid a visit to Bath. It is not recorded if she took the waters, but presumably some of her courtiers did. In 1590 she granted a new charter to the city, confirming the mayor and citizens' possession of the baths. Soon afterwards some of the dilapidated baths were restored, and in 1597 a hot-water bath for horses (advocated by Dr Turner a few decades earlier) was completed. However, the corporation running the enterprise seems to have been somewhat neglectful in its duties. As late as 1622 Bath was described as 'a verie little poore cittie'.[4]

By this time, however, Bath had hosted another monarch. Anne of Denmark, consort of King James I, visited Bath on three occasions, twice in 1613 and once in 1615. James, who had succeeded Elizabeth, was equally determined to create places for his subjects to take the waters free from contaminations of Catholicism (ironically, his wife was a secret convert to Catholicism). He too felt threatened by English Catholics, not least following the failed Gunpowder Plot in 1605. By 1612 all Englishmen wishing to visit Spa were forced to apply for a visa so they could be vetted, and they were made to swear the Oath of Allegiance before the pass was issued. The traffic across the Channel continued, and between 1613 and 1624 no fewer than 337 passes were granted to visit Spa.[5] The city and its holy well did indeed remain a hotbed of dissent. In 1615 the Pope authorized the English Catholics at Spa to choose an Archbishop of Canterbury, which they proceeded to do, provocatively electing Dr Thomas Worthington, president of the English College, a Catholic seminary in Douai.[6]

By the reign of James I, however, Spa's importance as a hotbed of Catholic dissent was being diluted. More and more Protestants, including prominent nobles, were going there to take the waters, or simply as part of their Grand Tour, and an Anglican chapel presently appeared in the town. Secondly, water from Spa was exported around Europe, with a large number of bottles making their way on the ten-day journey to England, thereby saving those with medical problems the difficulty of making their own journeys.[7] The virtues of the waters from Spa were promoted by English physicians, who soon began investigating the possibilities of more local sources. One proponent was the greatest English physician of the age, Dr William Paddy, president of the Royal College of Physicians 1609–11 and the personal physician of James I. The result was an enthusiasm on the part of landowners for sinking wells on their property, christening any natural spring as a 'spaw', and offering various amenities – usually rather primitive – to visitors in search of a cure but without sufficient funds to visit Bath or Spa. Over the next two centuries, more than 150 of these establishments (many short-lived) would appear around England. Word of these start-ups was spread by a new scientific literature, which featured titles such as *Newes out of Cheshire of the new found Well* (published in 1600) – whose author admitted in his preface that there were 'many incredible reportes' of wells being found – and *A True Report of certain Wonderful Overflowings in Somerset* (1607).

James was sympathetic to these entrepreneurial pursuits. He gave his blessing to a mineral spring on the Essex estate of one of his favourite courtiers, Mountjoy Blount. He made repeated visits to the establishment, ultimately christened Wanstead Spa, despite being warned by an advisor not to drink the waters, which had allegedly killed more than a few customers.[8]

One of the most successful of the new spas was developed 40 miles south of London, on the property in the Kent countryside of Edward Neville, Lord Abergavenny. In 1606 Lord Abergavenny was visited by a friend, a 24-year-old nobleman named Dudley, third Baron North. Lord North would suffer ill health and depression throughout his life. However, a quack preventative for the plague with which he dosed himself unsuccessfully in about 1604 did little to dent his enthusiasm for promising nostrums. He had drunk mineral waters at Spa in 1602, and four years later, while recuperating from illness at Lord Abergavenny's hunting lodge, he discovered the mineral springs. Since the nearest town was Tonbridge, the spa was duly christened 'the Tunbridge Wells'. It quickly achieved a measure of fame, its success based in part on the fact that it was considerably closer than Bath to London.

Tunbridge Wells offered little in the way of accommodation or other facilities, and throughout the seventeenth century visitors to the site – which was often difficult to access due to muddy roads in the Weald of Kent – were obliged to accommodate themselves in Tunbridge, 6 miles away. Others stayed slightly closer in the village of Rusthall, which by the middle of the century featured a pump room as well as bowling greens. The Tunbridge Wells itself consisted of little more than two small houses (one for men, another for women) in which the waters, served by a 'dipper', were drunk, along with, after 1638, a short promenade shaded by trees along which they could walk. For many years Tunbridge Wells featured a dipper named Mrs Humphreys, who died in 1678, reputedly at the age of 102 – a great advertisement for the healthy properties of the waters she ladled.

In 1632 a 'Doctor of Physick' from Ashford named Lodowick Rowzee published a treatise entitled *The Queen's Wells: That is, a Treatise of the Nature and Virtues of Tunbridge-Water. Together with an Enumeration of the chiefest Diseases, which it is good for; and against which*

it may be used; and the Manner and Order of taking it. It reported that the taste of the water was 'not unpleasant', though he admitted that some of those who drank it were purged by vomiting. His list of diseases for which it was effective included dropsy, jaundice, 'hard swelling of the spleen', kidney stones, 'clammy phlegmatic excrement bled in the bladder', palsy, vertigo, lethargy and various 'diseases of the head'.

Sadly, the water from the Tunbridge Wells seems to have done little for the man who discovered them, since Lord North once lamented: 'My whole life hath been but a conflict with the worst of diseases and a wearisome seeking for contentment, plunged in an irretrievable gulf of all misery.'[9] He nonetheless lived to the grand old age of 83, dying in 1666, by which time the Tunbridge Wells had been visited by Queen Henrietta Maria (in 1629) and her son, King Charles II (in 1663).

The first spa visited by Henrietta Maria on her arrival in England was not Tunbridge Wells, however, but Wellingborough in Northamptonshire, some 70 miles north of London. Wellingborough was a fashionable new establishment on one of the many properties (he owned thirty-two manors) of Fulke Greville, Lord Brooke. The well was discovered in 1624, and two years later Henrietta Maria, during her first full summer in England, spent nine weeks at Wellingborough. She returned the following summer, on which occasion she may well have briefly met a young gentleman from Huntingdonshire named Oliver Cromwell, who had also arrived to drink the waters, and who was treated by her physician, Sir Theodore Mayerne.[10] Less than twenty years later, in 1645, Cromwell would stop in Wellingborough with his New Model Army on his way to fight Henrietta Maria's husband, Charles I, at the Battle of Naseby.

A view of Tunbridge Wells from a 1719 engraving.

Epsom Well House, a 1796 watercolour by Christiana Rolle.

Another spa developed during the time of James I was at Epsom in Surrey. In the summer of 1618 a farmer named Henry Wicker discovered a small spring on his property. He enlarged the opening in hopes of using it to water his cattle, but the livestock obstinately refused to drink. The water was soon held to have curative properties, initially when applied topically to sores, then when it was drunk. It too was promoted by Lord North, who claimed he made its virtues, like those of the waters of the Tunbridge Wells, known to the 'citizens of London' because the journey to Spa was too costly and inconvenient for sick persons.[11] Epsom became a favoured resort of affluent Londoners, and as they travelled south on their way to the wells they were greeted in the village of Tooting by various hoteliers, tradesmen and quack doctors with eager requests for patronage. So insistent were the offers that the English word 'touting' comes from the village's name.[12]

The most successful new spa in the North was the one at
Harrogate, more specifically Knaresborough, a market town in the
West Riding of Yorkshire. There had already been a number of holy
wells in the area, such as St Magnus's and St Robert's, but in 1571
a new source of rust-coloured water, soon named the Tewit Well,
was discovered on the moor by William Slingsby. He brought the
waters to the attention of Queen Elizabeth's physician, Dr Timothy
Bright, who agreed that its medicinal properties equalled those of
Spa.

Harrogate, comprising the hamlets Knaresborough, High
Harrogate, Low Harrogate and Harlow Car, contained more than
ninety mineral springs. Due to the folding and faulting of the earth's
crust, these springs belong to the three main groups of mineral
waters – sulphurous (containing hydrogen sulfide), chalybeate or
ferruginous (impregnated with salts of iron) and saline (containing
a high concentration of sodium chloride). In the valley known as
Low Harrogate, locals bathed in a group of sulphur springs from
the early 1600s. However, Harrogate did not become popular or
successful until it was commended by an Oxford-trained physician
at York named Edmund Deane, who in 1626 published *Spadacrene
Anglica; or the English Spaw-Fountain*. Dr Deane saw the hand of God
at work here on the Yorkshire moors. 'See here,' he wrote, 'a most
admirable work guided by the omnipotency and wisdome of the
Almighty, that a naturall, clear, and pure water, should produce
so many and severall effects and operations.'[13] His catalogue of
the diseases for which it offered cures included catarrhs, palsies,
cramps, jaundice, kidney stones, haemorrhoids, headaches and
dizziness, and even 'cancarous tumours'. Visitors to the spa were,
however, obliged to put up with many inconveniences, since in the
early days there was no pump room or shelter, no lodgings, and – to
the dismay of the 'people of quality' – the presence of poor people

Harrogate became popular in the seventeenth century for its chalybeate, sulphurous and saline waters. Spa Well (site of Old Sulphur Well), Low Harrogate, 1829 engraving.

who left their putrid clothing lying around and washed their sores with the water that others were expected to drink.[14]

The wells of Harrogate became a popular destination nonetheless, and in the 1640s it was described as a 'great resort … by reason of the wells'.[15] The merits of using its sulphurous waters were publicized by Dr John French, a physician at London's Savoy Hospital and keen advocate of the use of spa water treatments for maimed soldiers. In 1651 he published *The Yorkshire Spaw*, whose subtitle advertised 'the Stinking or Sulphur Well'.[16] A visitor in 1664 left a description of the 'Sulphurus Spaw', noting that the water was 'of a most unpleasant smell and taste, and stinks like the smell of a sinke or rotten eggs, but is very medicinable for many deseases'.[17]

'MANY REMARKABLE CURES'

The English spas survived the political instability of the Civil Wars. Cromwell, who had visited Wellingborough in 1628, was advised to visit Bath for a cure in 1656. The hot baths had remained open throughout the turmoils, with wounded royalist soldiers often being treated in the waters.[18] At the Restoration, there were sixteen functioning spas in England. The royal patronage promptly continued. Charles II, like his mother Henrietta Maria, was an enthusiast for healing waters, having visited Bath in 1645 and Spa during his exile in 1654. Soon after his return to England in 1660 he went with his mother to Tunbridge Wells, and he would visit Epsom over the next few years as well.

The latter decades of the seventeenth century witnessed the decline of a number of existing spas, such as Wellingborough, and the discovery of other springs, such as the ones at Horwood in Buckinghamshire and Willowbridge in Staffordshire. At the latter, spa-goers not only drank the waters but also – despite the fact that they were cold – bathed in them. Willowbridge also offered a bath for horses. A pioneer in cold-water bathing was a certain Reverend

Fern from Matlock in Derbyshire, who, in about 1698, constructed a lead-lined bath in which members of the public could immerse themselves in waters from a spring discovered on the rugged dale.

In Yorkshire, the Middelton family cashed in on spa mania, building a circular, open-air plunge bath in 1699 at White Wells on Ilkley Moor. They also claimed that cold water treated all sorts of ailments, with Dr Joseph Browne, an advocate of cold-water bathing, asserting in his 1707 treatise *An Account of the Wonderful Cures performed by the Cold Baths* that they were responsible for 'many remarkable cures'. He was quick to blame luxurious living on why cold bathing was not popular: effeminate men preferred warm beds, spices, coffee, tea and chocolate, all of which, he claimed, weakened their constitutions. When a new landlord, Robert Dale, bought the land almost a century later in 1791, he replaced the original bath and built two separate outdoor ones. He advertised in the local newspaper that the waters healed sore eyes, tumours, scrofula and back problems. Donkeys carried patients up the steep path to the cottages. Tragically, in 1793 a 9-year-old girl named Anne Harper, the daughter of a local butcher, drowned in one of the baths.

Many of the spas that opened during the reign of James I but, for several decades, had offered only rudimentary facilities began to be developed in order to offer more appealing environs. Spas offered the aristocracy an opportunity to leave London, with its smells and crowds, during the summer months and yet continue, in the fresher air of the provinces, the kind of stimulating social interaction enjoyed in London during the other months of the year. Travel to these spas was made more comfortable by an improvement in the state of the roads, thanks to the efforts during the reign of Charles II, such as the Local Turnpike Act of 1663.

For those who left London, immersion in the waters at Bath, or drinking those in Epsom or Tunbridge Wells, became only part of the attraction. Many spas began offering more comfortable accommodation as well as musical performances and other entertainments. At Sissinghurst in Kent spa-goers could enjoy the large park owned by the Baker family, accommodation in their great Elizabethan mansion, local wines and ciders, fish extracted from the estate's ponds, and pastures in which to graze the horses which carried them from London. Alas, Tunbridge Wells provided too much competition, and Sissinghurst Spa, despite its pleasant amenities, quickly failed.[19]

One of the most successful spas by the end of the seventeenth century was that in Scarborough. Healing waters had first been discovered there in 1626 when a local woman, Thomasin Farrer, noticed russet-coloured waters bubbling out from the cliffs overlooking the sea. These waters soon gained a reputation for healing, thanks in large part to a physician, Robert Wittie, who published *Scarborough Spaw* in 1660. In 1698 a cistern was constructed to collect the waters. Celia Fiennes deplored the lack of amusements when she visited in 1697, but Scarborough had the advantage of beautiful scenery and a bracing climate, and many visitors extolled the delights of the views offered by the town, as well as the freshness of the sea breezes. 'Nothing can be more pleasing to the man of taste,' wrote one visitor, 'nothing more cheering to the broken-down spirits of the invalid, than this unique picture, which is, as it were, spread out before him at his very feet.'[20]

The spa waters at Scarborough were vulnerable to high tides, but so popular did it become that the corporation running Bath began spreading rumours that several eminent persons had died from drinking its waters. Fierce opposition also came from the proponents of Harrogate. However, the smears seem to have done little to endanger the popularity, and Scarborough Spa would later be crowned, by one writer, the 'Queen of English Watering Places'.[21] By the time of that confident pronouncement – the middle of the nineteenth century – there would be much competition for the title.

Other spas continued to be discovered and developed during the reigns of Charles II and James II. In 1684 workmen digging for coal at Butterby, near Durham, discovered a mineral spring, whose waters were quickly exploited. However, the economic future of the area would belong to coal rather than mineral water, and the waters disappeared with the sinking of collieries.

In 1665 the writer and antiquary John Aubrey discovered mineral waters on the property of his friend John Sumner (whose sister he was unsuccessfully courting) at Seend in Wiltshire, 15 miles east of Bath. After sending samples to the Royal Society in London two years later, Aubrey and Sumner began promoting the waters of their new spa. A house of entertainment duly appeared and bowling greens were laid out. However, the business ultimately failed because of its proximity to Bath.

Bath also faced competition from the mineral waters at Bristol Hotwells. From the 1400s, sailors claimed that the waters helped heal skin complaints, but it was William Worcester who, in 1480, first publicized them as warm and milky. Managing these waters was, however, always going to be troublesome. At high tide, seawater regularly polluted the spring at the bottom of St Vincent's Cliff. Despite the consort of Charles II, Queen Catherine of Braganza, endorsing the waters in 1677, it was not until 1696 that the Bristol Society of Merchants Venturers invested in the spring by building Hotwell House. Throughout the eighteenth century, visitors flitted between the spas of Bath and Bristol, but Hotwells fell into decline by the end of the century.

Bath would go from strength to strength throughout the eighteenth century, even after, 50 miles away, people in the small market town of Cheltenham noticed flocks of pigeons pecking at the salt deposits left by a spring near the town. Reckoning that pigeons couldn't be wrong, the townspeople began drinking the water to cure themselves of various ailments. The landowner, a Mr

Mason, railed off the site in 1718, raised a thatched roof over the well, added a bowling green, and, after experiments conducted by doctors from Worcester and Gloucester, began advertising the waters for their curative properties. By the 1740s his son-in-law, a retired Manx sea captain named Henry Skillicorne, expanded the enterprise. He deepened the well, raised a dome over it, installed a pump, and constructed a set of Assembly Rooms to host fashionable visitors. He had the building adorned with stone pigeons – a tribute to the creatures that discovered the waters, and that, fittingly, feature on the city's coat of arms.

Eighteenth-century engraving of Bristol Hotwells.

Mineral waters with supposedly beneficial qualities were also being discovered in London. In 1683 Thomas Sadler found an ancient holy well on his property in Clerkenwell. On the advice of a physician, he added beer to the water, then began bottling and selling his concoction. He also sweetened his mineral waters with a syrup. Sadler's Wells (sometimes known as 'New Tunbridge Wells' or 'Islington Spa') became such a thriving concern that it began stealing the custom of fashionable Londoners from Tunbridge Wells and Epsom. This popularity and prosperity were not to last, and by the end of the century Sadler's Wells was reduced to staging unsavoury spectacles (such as the 'Hibernian Cannibal', who ate a live cockerel onstage, feathers and all) to attract customers. By 1711 it was described as a 'nursery of debauchery'.[22]

Other spas grew up in London and its suburbs during the second half of the seventeenth century: in Acton, in Streatham, in Hampstead, and in the grounds of the Dog and Duck tavern in St George's Fields in Lambeth. This latter establishment prospered, and in the second half of the eighteenth century, known as 'St George's Spaw, Dog and Duck', it was run by a barmaid named Elizabeth Hedger. It featured skittles, a bowling green and baths for both men and women. The Dog and Duck ultimately received the blessing of none other than Samuel Johnson, who advised Mrs Thrale to take the waters there.

A drinking spa, or 'physic well', opened in Barnet, north of London, in the 1650s. It was visited by Samuel Pepys on 11 July 1664. He drank five glasses of water and, after relieving his bladder multiple times on the journey home, 'fell into a most mighty sweat in the night'. He was brave enough to return a few years later, when he took the precaution of drinking only three glasses. Afterwards he visited a local pub, the Red Lion, where he enjoyed 'some of the best cheese cakes I ever did eat in my life'.[23] Today his two visits to

Barnet are commemorated by a residential street, Pepys Crescent, which runs off Well Road.

The London spas were popular for Londoners because of their accessibility. They were frequented mainly by the poorer classes, who could not afford a coach or horse to transport them to establishments outside the city. Instead, they could walk to Hampstead, Sadler's Wells or across the river to Dulwich or Streatham. Daniel Defoe mused that 'the nobility and gentry go to *Tunbridge*, the Merchants and Rich Citizens to *Epsome*; so the Common People go chiefly to *Dullwich* and *Streatham*'.[24]

The majority of the wells developed over the course of the seventeenth century were drinking spas. However, cold-water bathing was becoming more popular. Besides Willowbridge, Ilkley and the Dog and Duck, one was developed in the heart of London, Coldbath Spa in Clerkenwell. In 1697 a spring was discovered here by a Mr Baynes, who began promoting in advertisements the virtues of bathing in cold water, claiming that it 'creates appetite, helps digestion, and makes hardy the tenderest constitution'. He constructed a gabled bathhouse complete with a large garden and four turreted summerhouses.[25]

At the dawn of the eighteenth century, spa mania flourished with the development of sixty spas throughout Britain. One could bathe in the naturally hot waters of Bath, Bristol Hotwells or the northern town of Buxton. The more adventurous could take a cold-water plunge in a rural spa or in the sea at Scarborough, or drink a glass of chalybeate, saline or sulphurous mineral water served by a professional dipper. As the eighteenth century dawned, the English spa was about to enter its 'golden age'. Repairing one's health would soon become secondary to socializing and taking advantage of other amenities on offer. Far from being uncivilized, a pursuit exclusive to the 'wild Irish' or the 'Red Indian', taking the waters would become a rite of passage for the elegant and sophisticated.

Places Observed by Letters

A	St James Church
B	the Abby Church
C	St Michaels Church
D	the Town Prison
E	the Free School
F	the Kings Bath
G	the Queens Bath
H	the Hot Bath
I	the Cross Bath
K	St Katherines Hospital
L	St Johns Hospital
M	Bridwel & Bridwel Lane
N	Vicarage Lane
O	Cock Lane
P	Nonhere Lane
Q	Gascoin's Tower
R	the Cock Pitt
S	Guild Hall

V the Meeting house
W Bear Corner
T St Johns Chapel

GreatKings Mead

through Caursham

Avon flu

Little Kings Mead

the Ambrey

Burr Wall

Bristol Road

Froom Road

the bridge

South Gate Street

South Gate

Stauls Stre

Ham Gate

A Leer

Lane

Abby Green

The Ham

Abbey Gard

Sold by Tho Taylor at ye Golden Lyon in Fleet Street

Jo Savage Sculp

ⲤⲎ OF BATH

Barton Ground

Brystol Road

West Gate

Fives
Court

Timber Green

West Gate Street

Bear Inn

New
Bowling
Green

the Way to London

Cheap Street

Brad Street

Walcot Street

High Street

North Gate

Avon flu

Bathwick mill

Bathwick Mead

vision is 66 feet or 22 Yards
illmore delin: Teacher of ỿ Mathematicks
in Bristoll

The South Side of the Abby Church

THREE

Bladud's Realm

BEAU NASH AND
THE DEVELOPMENT OF BATH

Bath was the exemplar of this revolution in bathing, health and socializing. Yet anyone arriving to take the waters in Bath during the sixteenth or seventeenth centuries would have been in for a rude awakening. The city might have been wealthy in comparison to many other cities, but it was still filthy and smelly. 'All kinds of disorders were grown to their highest Pitch in Bath', the architect John Wood the Younger wrote of the city in the mid-1600s,

> insomuch as the streets and public ways of the City were become like so many Dunghills, Slaughter-Houses, and Pig-Styes: For Soil of all sorts, and even Carrion, was cast and laid in the streets, and the Pigs turned out by Day to feed and route among it.[1]

Besides the rotting rubbish and manure from horses and cattle, the streets also swam with the contents of chamber pots thrown from the windows of houses by those who declined to use the designated 'bum ditch' outside the city walls. Brewers, butchers, chandlers, soap-boilers and tanners polluted the air as well as the streets. Little wonder that nosegays of sweet-smelling herbs were offered to visitors on arrival.

This muck and mayhem had not deterred visitors. Indeed, so many people came for relief, often the sick and diseased, that the

PREVIOUS SPREAD A map from John Savage's *The City of Bath*, c.1697.

Corporation of Bath, which had run the city and its almshouses since the dissolution of Bath Priory in 1539, sought help from Parliament. The Poor Relief Act was passed in 1572, forbidding any 'diseased or impotent' person from visiting Bath unless two justices from his native county gave him a licence to do so. This licence guaranteed that the patient's parish would financially support the patient during his or her stay. Failure to produce a licence at the city gates was met with a harsh punishment, for the offender would be branded on his chest with a hot iron with a *V* for vagabond and given a punishment of two years of unpaid work for a local farmer.[2]

Once inside the gates of the city, the visitors faced other problems. Not only were the streets in poor condition, but the city's hostelries were grubby and few and far between. Very few new homes were built in the century between 1592 and 1692 – a mere seventeen. Such lodgings as there were featured floors sticky with soot and beer, as well as coarse bed linen hosting the inevitable bedbugs, ensuring the guest a restless night of scratching and itching.

Other amenities were equally disappointing. Entertainment was basic, such as the open-air dancing on a bowling green where a 'fiddle and a hautboy formed the whole band'.[3] Inclement weather would immediately halt proceedings. A sycamore grove, popular for promenades, was unsafe for women. Street football, bear-baiting and cockfighting were all too common a sight. But all of these vulgar entertainments were soon to be replaced by more refined diversions.

THE MASTER OF CEREMONIES

The man responsible for initiating Bath's dramatic metamorphosis was a charismatic man about town, easily recognizable from the distinctive white hat that became his trademark: Richard Nash, known as Beau despite the fact that, as someone unkindly remarked, he was 'a very ugly man'.[4] Born in Swansea in October 1674, Nash was the son of a glassmaker, although he never publicly discussed his family or childhood. When Sarah, the Duchess of Marlborough, teased him about his reticence, comparing him to the fictional Gil Blas, who was ashamed of his father,[5] Nash replied: 'No, madam, I seldom mention my father in company; not because I have any reason to be ashamed of him, but because he has some reason to be ashamed of me.'[6] There was probably more than a little truth in this statement.

Nash was educated at a grammar school in Carmarthen and then at Jesus College, Oxford, but studying was never his forte. Instead, he showed a precocious interest in gambling and womanizing. At 17, in Oxford, he asked a local woman to marry him, but the engagement terminated when he fled the city with unpaid debts. He persuaded his father to purchase a commission in the army for him, but the life of a soldier did not suit him, although he gloried in the uniform – a hint of the flamboyant persona that was to come. His next career move, as a law student at the Middle Temple, proved no more successful, although he continued his campaign of socializing and pleasure-seeking, dressing smartly and funding his lifestyle through gambling and from borrowing money from friends. By the age of 30 he had become successful as a professional gamester. He spent the winters gaming in London and the summers on the Continent at places known for gambling such as Aix-les-Bains, Spa, and The Hague.

Nash's first attempt at organizing a high-profile social event had been while he was still a student at the Middle Temple. The Inns of Court offered students opportunities beyond legal instruction. England's kings and queens had long been entertained with masques, pageants, banquets and jousts arranged by organizations such as London's lord mayor and aldermen. Among the many companies performing for their highnesses' pleasure were the masquers of the four Inns of Court – Middle Temple, Inner Temple, Gray's Inn and Lincoln's Inn – in whose halls plays and other entertainments had been staged at least since the time of Henry VIII. In 1695 the 21-year-old Nash volunteered to take on the organizational task of putting on a masque in Middle Temple Hall for King William III, complete with music, dancing, singing and acting. He did such a stellar job that, according to his biographer Oliver Goldsmith, the king allegedly offered Nash a knighthood, which Nash politely turned down – although he was bold enough to hint that he would accept the offer of an appointment as a 'Knight of Windsor', a post that would have come with a pension as well as accommodation in Windsor Castle. The king did not take the hint.

Nash probably became aware of Bath's potential as a resort after learning of how the shy, puffy and short-sighted Queen Anne, seeking relief from gout, paid a visit to the city in 1702 and again in 1703. The Corporation of Bath enthusiastically welcomed their royal guest, who was accompanied by her husband, Prince George of Denmark, as well as her courtiers and various fashionable guests. As the queen reached the city gates, she was greeted by two hundred virgins dressed as Amazons armed with bows and arrows. Dancers frolicked beside her coach, and at the West Gate the mayor and various dignitaries of the Corporation received her. As she entered the city, the queen touched

Queen Anne depicted in an enamel miniature by Charles Boit, c. 1705.

Bath Pump Room viewed from the front. Undated engraving, mid-eighteenth century.

the necks of thirty unfortunate scrofula sufferers who believed the monarch's touch — what was known as the 'royal touch' — would cure them of this affliction, known as the 'King's evil'.

Nash arrived in Bath soon afterwards, in 1704, and he immediately put himself forward as the right-hand man of Captain Thomas Webster, a fellow gamester and the unofficial organizer of dances at the town hall.[7] Guests paid half a guinea to attend one of these dances, which were hardly the elegant balls for which Bath was soon to become famous under Nash. There were no rules and regulations to ensure polite behaviour, smoking was permitted, gentlemen could wear their heavy boots, and women, disdaining fashionable dress, appeared in white aprons. Drunkenness and duelling were common. Indeed, duelling claimed a high-profile victim when, in 1705, Captain Webster died following a dispute over a debt from a game of cards.

Webster's demise meant the way was clear for Nash to take over as master of revels. With his experience of organizing social events in London, and having learned about the entertainments in Bath under Webster, Nash was appointed the new Master of Ceremonies. He looked every inch the part, always wearing a bejewelled black wig (not the usual powdered grey), a beaver-trimmed hat tipped at a rakish angle, and a braided coat deliberately left open to expose his waistcoat and ruffled shirt.

Under the charter granted by Elizabeth I in 1590, Bath was administered by the Corporation of Bath, a self-selecting body of councillors, aldermen and a mayor. Nash's appointment as Master of Ceremonies coincided with changes that the Corporation was initiating to transform it from a place of convalescence – a city attracting the sick and the lame – to a place with much broader appeal. In the early seventeenth century the local aristocracy sponsored visiting acting companies for entertainment, hiring the town hall or inn yards for them to perform in. These performances, however, were organized on an ad hoc basis. Not until a new playhouse opened in Trim Street in 1705 – the same year, coincidentally, that Nash became Master of Ceremonies – did a theatre become a permanent fixture and an added attraction for visitors.[8]

A year later the purpose-built Pump Room was completed, designed by John Wood and commissioned by the royal physician, William Oliver. Orchestras now had a venue to entertain visitors while they sipped the mineral waters and observed, through a window, the bathers in the King's Bath. Oliver strongly advocated drinking the waters as well as bathing in them, backing up his arguments with scientific facts.

Another issue for Nash and the Corporation to address was transportation links. Bath had been notoriously difficult for visitors to reach. A stagecoach took three days to travel the 100 miles from London, and the venture was costly and uncomfortable as well as time-consuming. As Edward Ward lamented in 1700, the road to Bath was 'rocky, unloved and narrow', and he speculated that 'the Alps are to be passed with less danger'. He complained of being 'jolted so cursedly, that I thought it would have made a Dislocation of my Bones'.[9] There was a movement to improve roads within London from 1660, and the Turnpike Acts of 1663 and 1695 gave powers for the collection of tolls for the construction and maintenance of principal roads. The Bath Corporation, fortunately, recognized that the only way to attract visitors was to improve roads to and within the city. The Bath Turnpike Trust was accordingly created in 1707, intended to lure visitors from London to the lavish entertainments Nash and the Corporation were preparing for them.

RULES TO BE OBSERV'D AT BATH

Nash's first act as Bath's Master of Ceremonies was to organize a music subscription – a fee of 1 guinea to raise funds to support a band of six performers. Within two years, he had raised nearly £1,800, a considerable sum. In the meantime, the Corporation laid proper roads, paved streets and provided lighting. Plans were afoot for the building of more lodgings to house visitors. There was, however, still nowhere to play cards, or for polite society to drink tea, coffee or chocolate. Nash therefore encouraged a local builder, Thomas Harrison, to erect the Assembly Rooms between Bath Abbey and North Parade. In 1708 the first visitors were welcomed through the doors.[10] When subscriptions were raised to 2 guineas, even finer facilities became possible, such as gardens for promenades, and a larger band was hired. Even so, the satirists did not spare the new Assembly Rooms, in particular taking it to task for its gaming and its outlandish fashions – the fops in scarlet stockings and the 'Tissue Shoes', the heads 'adorn'd with Brussel's Lace', the 'Powder'd Lobster in the Edg'd Hat'.[11] It was in this flamboyant company, however, that Nash would reign supreme.

Different social classes mixed together in Bath. Expanding trade and increased prosperity meant that England's 'middling sort' – prosperous merchants, physicians and lawyers, from London as well as other cities and towns – became avid consumers of recreational activities. At balls and concerts in Bath, they came into social contact with the more aristocratic and courtly visitors. Indeed, Nash fostered this kind of mixing, discouraging private parties and thereby enabling the middle classes the opportunity of mingling with the aristocracy. If the latter needed to refine their often violent and disorderly behaviour, such as duelling, the middle classes, not yet socially sure-footed, required some assurance about

Richard ('Beau') Nash (1674-1761). Oil on canvas, based on a work of c. 1761 by William Hoare.

the rules of engagement. Recognizing that polite behaviour was necessary to avoid the drunkenness, social lapses and fashion faux pas that had previously characterized the town, Nash posted a series of rules in the Pump Room in 1707. During their stay, visitors were obliged to observe these 'Rules to be observ'd at Bath'.

The Laws of Bath
By general Consent determin'd

I.

THAT a Visit of Ceremony at coming BATH, and another at going away, is all that is expected, or desired by Ladies of Quality and Fashion; —*except Impertinents.*

II.

THAT Ladies coming to Ball, appoint a Time for their Footmen's coming to wait on them Home; to prevent Disturbances and Inconveniencies to themselves and others.

III.

THAT Gentlemen of Fashion never appearing in a Morning before the Ladies in Gowns and Caps, shew Breeding and Respect.

IV.

THAT Gentlemen coming into the Rooms in Boots, where Ladies are, shew their little Regards to them or Company; —*except they have no Shoes.*

V.

THAT no Person take it ill that any one goes to another's Play, or Breakfast, and not to theirs; —*except captious by Nature.*

VI.

THAT no Gentleman give his Ticket for the Balls to any but Gentlewomen. —*N.B.* Unless he has none of his Acquaintance.

VII.

THAT Gentlemen crowding before Ladies at the Ball, shew ill Manners; and that none do so for the Future; —*except such as respect No-body but themselves.*

VIII.

THAT no Gentleman or Lady take it ill that another dances before them; —*except such as have no Pretence to dance at all.*

IX.

THAT Ladies dressing and behaving like Handmaids, must not be surprised if they are treated as Handmaids.

X.

THAT the elder Ladies and Children be content with a second Bench at the Ball, as being past, or not come to Perfection.

XI.

THAT the younger Ladies take Notice how many Eyes observe them. —*N.B.* This does not extend to *Have-at-Alls.*

XII.

THAT all Whisperers Lies and Scandal be taken for their Authors and that all Repeaters of such Lies and Scandal be shunn'd by all Company;—*except such as have been guilty of the same Crime.*

☞ *Several Men of no Character, Old Women and Young Ones, of question'd Reputation, are great Authors of Lies in this Place, being of the Sect of Levellers.*

———

Whereas POLITENESS, DECENCY, and GOOD-MANNERS, three ancient Residents at BATH, have, of late, left the Place; whoever shall restore them, shall be rewarded with *Honour* and *Respect.*

RICHARD NASH
Master of the Ceremonies
The Pump Room, Bath 1707

Although many courtesy books giving rules of social conduct had already been published, they were primarily aimed at aristocrats and courtiers, such as Laurence Humphrey's *The Nobles, or of Nobilitye* (1563) and Richard Brathwaite's *The English Gentleman* (1630) and *The English Gentlewoman* (1631). Nash's rules treated the social classes more equally and inclusively. Furthermore, his code of conduct was not merely a series of suggestions: no deviation from the rules was tolerated. Crucially, it represented one of the first attempts to formally structure social etiquette, ensuring safe and enjoyable interaction between the classes and the sexes. It would soon be copied, in spas throughout the country, spreading a gospel of good manners. As Goldsmith wrote, the gentry brought back to London the 'ease and open access' they had first acquired at Bath, 'and thus the whole kingdom by degrees became more refined'.[12]

'Ladies of Quality and Fashion', Nash stipulated, were required to prearrange a time for their footmen to collect them in the evening. This rule was intended to prevent 'disturbances and inconveniences to themselves and others'. Meanwhile, 'Gentlemen of Fashion' were instructed to show 'breeding and respect' before the ladies, such as always appearing in appropriate attire and never crowding them at the ball. Gossip and scandal were strictly forbidden, with 'whisperers of lies and scandal' to be shunned by the company. This rule carried a special observation: 'Several Men of no Character, Old Women and Young Ones of Question'd Reputation, are great authors of Lies in this Place, being of the sect of Levellers.'[13] The ban appears to have done little good: in 1725, in *Bath Intrigues*, Eliza Haywood wrote that if you wished to hear gossip a 'thousand Tongues are ready to oblige you'. As she pointed out: 'If a Person has a mind to have his Character, Humour, Circumstances, nay, those of his great Grandfather repeated, let him come to the Bath.'[14]

One of Nash's other preoccupations was with dress. He introduced a dress code at his balls after waging a successful battle against men wearing heavy boots and swords. The latter, he lamented, tore at women's dresses, although banning swords actually had more to do with avoiding duels over gambling or women – the fate that had overtaken his predecessor. Indeed, the banning of swords was so successful that in Richard Brinsley Sheridan's 1775 play *The Rivals* Captain Absolute mutters under his breath 'A Sword seen in the streets of Bath would raise as great an alarm as a mad dog.'[15] The observation was ironic considering that Sheridan fought two duels with a sword.

Meanwhile, to prevent men from wearing inappropriate footwear such as heavy boots, Nash wrote a poem entitled 'Frontinella's Invitation to the Assembly':

'Come one and all, to Hoyden Hall,
For there's the assembly this night;
    None but Servile fools
    Mind manners and rules;
We Hoydens do decency slight.

'Come trollops and slatterns,
Cock'd hats and white aprons,
This best our modesty suits;
    For why should not we
    In dress be as free
As Hogs-Norton squires in boots?'[16]

Nash also produced a puppet show to emphasize his dislike of boots. Punch and Judy puppet shows arrived from Italy during the seventeenth century, and in Nash's version Punch bursts onto the scene, booted and spurred like a country squire, so attached to his boots that he even wears them to bed. Judy pleads for him to take them off. Punch refuses. 'My boots,' he replies, 'why Madam, you might as well pull off my legs! I never go without boots; I never ride, I never dance, without them; and this piece of politeness is quite the thing in Bath.' His wife is so fed up with him and his boots that she kicks him offstage to the roars of laughter and applause from the crowd.[17]

If the visitors needed to be suitably attired, so too did Bath itself. During the eighteenth century the city was given a makeover. Nash worked alongside the Corporation to turn Bath into a visually attractive city. Bath was blessed with a beautiful local limestone, golden in colour, in use for at least a century before Nash's arrival. However, a Cornishman named Ralph Allen, a younger contemporary of Nash, was largely responsible for exploiting Bath stone to create many of the city's beautiful buildings. After making his fortune developing a national postal system, Allen acquired the quarries at Combe Down and Bathampton Down mines. While constructing his elegant mansion, Prior Park, as a showpiece for Bath stone, he designed an original wooden railway and cranes that made possible the transportation of huge, honeyed stones. Stone from Allen's quarries came to adorn buildings in Bath, including historic structures such as the Hot Bath (built in 1775), the Cross Bath (1784) and the Pump Room, originally built in 1745 and replaced in 1796. Allen even donated building stone from his mines for the construction of the Bath General Hospital that opened in 1742. He served as mayor of Bath in that same year, and in the following decade he served for a number of years as the city's Member of Parliament – one of Nash's few rivals in terms of power and influence.

THE KING OF BATH

Nash was described by one admirer as the 'life and soul of all ... diversions. Without him there is no play or assembly nor ball.'[18] His success as Master of Ceremonies was due to his ability to gauge fashions and moods. His progressive vision for initiating new trends and offering high-quality social diversions would soon be copied in spas throughout Britain. His flamboyant and charismatic nature allowed him to persuade the Corporation that he alone should be entrusted with providing entertainment for the visitors of Bath. He insisted the spa would be commercially successful, and he was proved correct as visitors flocked to his dances and enjoyed the dizzy whirl of his diversions. A dozen years after his arrival, in 1716, Nash was awarded the Freedom of the City. He soon became known as the 'King of Bath'.

Not everyone was enamoured of Nash's success. The poet Robert Whatley complained that the Master of Ceremonies enjoyed 'a Power that is wholly despotick ... Your Word is your Law; and whatever Mr N pleases to order, every one submits to with the same Pleasure and Resignation.'[19] Indeed, Nash's sense of his own importance knew no bounds. He once rebuked the Duchess of Queensberry for wearing an apron, and on another occasion he forbade Princess Amelia, the daughter of King George II, from dancing after 11 p.m. – the time at which all dancing and music ceased. He could be rude, obstinate, obnoxious and, to those who violated his rules, cruel and spiteful.

Such was his vanity that in 1741 Nash presented the Corporation with his portrait, painted by the artist William Hoare. It was hung in the Assembly Rooms between the busts of two illustrious figures, Sir Isaac Newton and Alexander Pope.[20] Not everyone was a fan of the 'King of Bath' or saw this placement as fitting.

It was not long before the 'King of Bath' set his sights on expanding his empire. His first target was Tunbridge Wells, a spa easily accessible from London. One minor problem stood in his way, a woman named Bell Causey, the incumbent Master of Ceremonies. She was no ordinary woman, taking charge in 1725 'as absolute governess'.[21] It was a rise in fortune for a woman who began her career dressing as a nymph and selling oranges and nosegays at the Ring in Hyde Park.

The season at Bath originally ran from late October until Christmas, with a slightly less fashionable season from late January to June. However, the two seasons ultimately merged, which meant Bath was a fashionable retreat for ten months of the year. Tunbridge's season was June, July and August, sandwiched between the two seasons at Bath. There should therefore have been no reason for competition between the two spas, all the more so since their clientele were quite different. Tunbridge, nearer to London, attracted a more varied demographic, a mixture of continental nobility and diplomats, who mixed with merchants. Bell had made herself an extremely popular mistress of the revels, organizing small gatherings, gambling and any other entertainments requested. After chapel, she waited on the steps leading to the walks for the visitors, gently hustling them 'as they do chickens, to any place, and for any purpose she wanted them for'. One shop owner described how she treated them with jellies, oranges and biscuits, and gave leftovers to the poor, 'by whom she was adored'.[22]

Bell, who disliked Nash, was understandably eager to protect her position in Tunbridge Wells. Despite her efforts to make Nash feel unwelcome, the 'King of Bath' always arrived in Tunbridge in a chariot pulled by five grey horses, complete with outriders, footmen and the sound of French horns. To show his outrage at not being treated with the respect he thought his due, Nash feigned disgust after the first ball, making a huge show of departing immediately for Bath. Bell was left fuming. But sadly, after a nine-year reign, Bell died unexpectedly in 1734. Nash, benefiting once again from a sudden demise, lost no time in taking over her role. He was later aptly described as creating a kingdom in Bath and 'sending off Tunbridge as one of its colonies'.[23] His reign at Tunbridge Wells would, however, witness an improvement in both the facilities and the entertainments.

4 Mr. Cibber (Colley)
5 Mr. Garrick
6 Mrs. Frasi (The Singer)
7 Mr. Nash.

8 Miss Chudleig b. (Duch.ss of Kingston)
9 Mr. Pitt. (Earl of Chatham)
10 Mr. Onslow (The Speaker)
11 Ld. Powi.

12 Dutch.ss of Norfolk
13 Miss Banks
14 Lady Lincoln
15 Mr. Littelton (Afterwards Lord Lyttleton)

16 The Baron (A German Canceller)
17 Anonym. (Mr. Richardson)
18 Mrs. Onslow

19 Miss Onslow
20 Mrs. Johnson (The B...)
21 Mr. Whiston.

Printed 20th May 1804 for Richard Phillips Nr. St Pauls Church Yard.

The remarkable characters who were at Tunbridge Wells with Richardson in 1748.
The illustration shows Samuel Richardson and friends such as Samuel Johnson, the actor David Garrick and the Earl of Chatham.

Nash never married, although in the course of his long career he had relationships with the celebrated beauty Fanny Murray, with an innkeeper's daughter named Juliana Popjoy, and with a 'termagant Woman' known only as Mrs Hill.[24] He enjoyed a long life, keeping up appearances as much as possible despite increasingly slender means. Sadly, his old age was not a happy one. A lifetime of excess eventually left him immobile, with boils on his legs (which the waters of Bath evidently failed to cure). His biographer, Goldsmith, claimed that he was 'past the power of giving or receiving pleasure, for he was poor, old and peevish'.[25] As the years passed, he lost his charm as well as his health, becoming even ruder and more abrasive, with people growing less tolerant of his tyrannical behaviour. As he increasingly became an embarrassment, the Corporation became anxious to relieve him of his post, although it agreed to a pension of 10 guineas paid on the first Monday of each month. The sum kept him from starvation and the poorhouse but was hardly enough for him to keep up the extravagant social life that once made him so famous. It was a sad end for a man who for so long bestrode Bath and Tunbridge Wells, his cane held like a sceptre and his white hat worn like a crown. After he died in 1762, at the grand age of 88, the Corporation paid £50 for his burial. He was given an appropriately lavish send-off, with a funeral procession to Bath Abbey from his house in Saw Close, complete with clergy, musicians, aldermen and proprietors of the Assembly Rooms, along with hospital patients and children from the charity school. His final resting place is beneath pew 33 in the abbey's nave.

After Nash's death, various people vied to take over his position as Master of Ceremonies. Ironically, the post intended to maintain civility and order in Bath became a source of dispute and disorder in 1768, as a poem entitled 'The Two Kings of Bath' recounted:

Of whom hereafter may be KING
Of *Bladud's* Realm, where Mirth should reign,
But Discord now the Waters stain;
That Place, where *Venus* should preside,
The fiery *Mars* does seem to guide.[26]

The contenders for the post were a Major Brereton and a Mr Plomer, the latter of whom had been the Master of Ceremonies at Bristol Hotwells. Plomer was duly elected, leaving Brereton's supporters furious. Bath remained deeply divided, with angry exchanges of pamphlets, poems and occasionally fisticuffs. At Plomer's first official engagement, opponents dragged him from the Assembly Rooms by the nose. Further brawling and hair-pulling followed, with women's dresses apparently torn to shreds. The mayor was summoned and forced to read the Riot Act three times before the fracas died down. 'Never was such a Scene of Anarchy and Confusion remembered in this City, as happened on Tuesday Night last', the *Bath Chronicle* reported.[27] Residents must have looked back fondly on the reign of the first King of Bath.

Beau Nash established at Bath a model of refined recreational diversions that other spas were eager to replicate. Spas throughout the country quickly adopted many of his measures – his rules of etiquette and his subscription-based entertainments, which included balls and pleasure gardens as well as health-giving waters – to create polite and civilized social gatherings. Masters of Ceremony were hired in spas throughout the land and given similarly influential powers over their resorts.

Which resorts succeeded would depend on a number of factors. There was no shortage of opportunity. In 1740 the Scottish physician Thomas Short, who created a cure for dysentery, listed 228 mineral wells in Britain.[28] Only a handful of these would develop into spa resorts, with the majority remaining small medicinal wells for locals before drying up and disappearing. For a spa to achieve the status of a resort such as Bath or Tunbridge Wells it needed precisely the sorts of features that Nash and the Corporation worked so hard to realize at Bath: ease of accessibility, quality accommodation and entertainments, and appropriate facilities – including, of course, waters whose benefits the local physicians and, if possible, celebrity and even royal visitors would extol. To the victor would go Nash's beaver-trimmed crown.

FOUR

Sense of Humours

BATHING AND DRINKING THE WATERS

A decade or so before Beau Nash arrived in Bath, a man named Edward Washbeare came to town seeking a cure. A Londoner who suffered from palsy, he came 'creeping on his hands and knees'. He was given a course of treatment by a physician named Thomas Guidott, who later published an account of cures performed, and benefit received, 'by the use of the famous hot waters of Bath'. After ten weeks of treatment in the baths, Mr Washbeare made a remarkable recovery.[1] Dr Guidott's condition also improved, for he began receiving referrals from hospitals in Bristol, Gloucester and even as far away as London.

In *An Essay on Bath Waters*, published in 1770, William Falconer claimed, probably with no great exaggeration, that 'upwards of a thousand Treatises' had been published on the medical virtues of water.[2] Most of these needed to be taken with the proverbial pinch of salt. Two decades later another author wrote that these accounts 'are very little to be depended on, as they are mostly filled with instances of the grossest ignorance, or misrepresentation'.[3] Many of these treatises contained more promotion and publicity than science.

William Hoare, *Dr. Oliver and Mr. Peirce, the First Physician and Surgeon Examining Patients Inflicted with Paralysis, Rheumatism and Leprosy*, 1761.

The Circus, 1773, etching by J.R. Cozens showing sedan and bath chairs, in *8 Views of the most elegant scenes of and in Bath*.

Even so, a wealth of anecdotal evidence no doubt existed for successful treatments, and a number of the claims made for spa waters, taken both internally and externally, have been borne out by recent scientific studies into conditions such as gout, lead poisoning and chlorosis.

We can easily understand the credulity of spa-goers in an era when medical science understood disease so imperfectly, when one could die from a simple infection, when plague, cholera and dysentery killed off large numbers of the population, and when

people suffered from the myriad ailments catalogued with gruesome
thoroughness by authors such as Dr Rouse. Their faith in the water
cures had been shaped not only by the example of those, such as
Edward Washbeare, who had evidently been healed by a regime
of sipping thermal water from a spring. They also had the ancient
beliefs and experiences of their ancestors at the holy wells dedicated
to saints. Even Dr Rouse's treatise carried on its title page the
assertion that medicinal waters had been bestowed on mankind by
the 'God of Nature'. Science may have replaced superstition, but the
healing waters, for most spa-goers, still moved in mysterious ways.
And it was this faith that induced them to plunge into the sulphurous waters and then drink them in the Pump Room.

Robins, Pinx.^t   A View of the KING and QUEEN'S Bath

Under the Statue of King Bladud, in the Niche on the Right hand, this Inscription
great Philosopher & Mathematician, bred at Athens, & Recorded the first discoverer & fo
Pump are the following lines placed { Jehovah's Blessings let's Admire, | Bethesdas Pool by
                                      Here's constant Heat & yet no Fire, | Hither remov'd to

...g the Great *PUMP-ROOM* at *BATH*. *W.ᵗ Elliott Sculpᵗ*

...e year 1669, — *Bladud Son of Lud-hudibras, Eighth King of the Britons from Brute a*
...*Baths, 863 years before Christ, that is 2562 years to the year 1699, and over the Common*

God and the King are our free imparters,	
God gives the Waters, the King the Charters.	printed for I. Kitchin at Nᵒ 59 Holborn Hill London.

For many centuries, European medicine was governed by this concept of the four humours (from the Latin *umor*, 'liquid'). Derived from the Greek Hippocrates and developed by the second-century Roman physician Galen, this theory divided bodily fluids into four distinct substances: blood, bile, phlegm and choler. An excess of or deficiency in any of them affected an individual's health and temperament. Physicians since ancient times believed most diseases were caused by an excess of one of these fluids, of which the body needed to rid itself through actions such as sweating, vomiting, defecating, reducing food intake or – that favourite medical procedure – bloodletting.

Precisely how illness worked was described by a Southampton physician, John Speed, in a 1750 treatise. If not hereditary, an illness developed and progressed because of obstructed perspiration that caused the stomach's digestive powers to 'grow languid'. Food was therefore inadequately digested such that a phlegm adhered to the stomach and intestines, preventing secretions from the 'intestinal glands' and causing 'a crude chyle' – the fatty fluids in the small intestine – to enter the blood. The presence of the chyle affected the temperature of the blood and consequently both its circulation and 'the secretion of the humours through the glands of the whole body … and of the nervous fluid by the brain'. Treatment therefore needed to restore perspiration as well as digestion; the phlegm needed to be forced 'downward' and the humours returned to their natural state.[4] Water was regarded as a particularly effective means of achieving these ends. Bathing in certain types of water could restore perspiration. Meanwhile, drinking water aided the removal of the phlegm by inducing vomiting, urination and defecation – the holy trinity of 'the purge'.

PREVIOUS PAGES *A View of the King and Queen's Baths, including the Great Pump Room in Bath.* Engraved in 1764 after a 1747 drawing by Thomas Robins.

A DIP IN THE WATERS

For those taking the waters at Bath, mornings began early. The baths were open between the hours of six and nine in the morning. Guests were picked up from their lodgings and transported directly to the baths in sedan chairs. John Macky, a Scottish spy and travel writer, described his experience: 'The chairmen, whatever storey you sleep in, come to one's bedside, strip you, give you their dress, wrap you in blankets, carry you off. And then after bathing, you are carried home.'[5] In 1687 Celia Fiennes described her experience of being conveyed to the baths in 'a low seate and with frames round and over your head, and all cover'd inside and out with red bayes and a curtain drawn before of the same which makes it close and warme'.[6]

Guests were deposited at one of the five baths in town, all of them open to the sky, in bad repair, and difficult to reach via narrow passages known as 'slips'. The approach to the baths was therefore ominous and unsettling. One doctor complained that 'the avenues which lead to the Slips are dark narrow passages, less conspicuous by far than the entrances to the meanest inns. The Slips resemble cells rather for the dead than dressing-rooms to the living.'[7] Those of means enjoyed the King's and the Cross Baths. The latter was extremely small, measuring only 20 feet long by 19 feet wide, but according to the diarist Samuel Pepys it gained its nickname – the 'pleasure bath' – thanks to its popularity with the gentry. Grateful bathers donated brass rings to be attached to the walls for bathers to hold on to. The first was donated in 1612 by Lydia White, daughter of a London draper. Charles II's mistresses, the duchesses of Cleveland and Portsmouth, also donated rings.

The fact that the baths were open to the heavens, as well as surrounded by high buildings, meant bathing was something of a spectator sport. In 1705, the year Beau Nash became Master of Ceremonies, Samuel Gale published his *A Tour Through Sev'ral Parts of England*, which included an account of his visit to Bath.

'The situation of the baths is promiscuous,' he wrote, describing how 'spectators from the windows may view the company when bathing'. At least, he noted, the bathers were meant to be dressed 'in their proper habits', which they donned in their lodgings. The men wore 'fine canvas waistcoats', as well as canvas drawers, slippers and a linen cap, while the women appeared in 'canvas gown and petticoats with pieces of lead affixed at the bottom, to keep them down under the water'. Thus attired, often with morning gowns (for warmth and modesty) thrown over the costume, the bathers were conducted to the baths in sedan chairs.[8]

Celia Fiennes described the practice whereby women hired two female water-guides for their bathing sessions. A guide at each elbow chaperoned their charge, keeping her upright while in the water. 'The Ladye goes into the bath with garments made of a fine yellow canvas, which is stiff and made large with great sleeves like a parsons gown, the water fills it up so that its borne off that your shape is not seen, it does not cling close as other linning which lookes sadly in the poorer sort that go in their own linning.'[9]

The perils of bathing in this cumbersome attire were comically described in *The Expedition of Humphry Clinker*, in which the servant, Winnifred, is threatened with a laxative, 'a dose of bumtaffy', unless she agrees to accompany her mistress to the baths. While in the water she experiences a mortifying accident when her petticoat accidentally comes off. Luckily, she reports, 'they could see nothing; for I was up to the sin in water'.[10] There must have been many such wardrobe malfunctions, although the lead weights described by Gale no doubt saved the modesty of many a bather. Fortunately for Winnifred and anyone else suffering similar mishaps, the Corporation employed a watchful sergeant to ensure that males and females kept what Fiennes called 'their due distance'.[11]

The mingling of sexes in the baths was always a pressing matter of concern. In 1562 Dr William Turner, an advocate for mineral baths, urged a ban on mixed bathing, arguing for separate baths for women. Accordingly, the Women's Bath – ultimately rechristened the Queen's Bath following Anne's visit – was single-sex, but mixed bathing continued in the other baths. Recommendations were made in 1621 for segregation in the Cross Bath, although no action was taken. But in 1625 the Privy Council lamented that 'great disorder' and 'very unseemly and immodest' behaviour continued to occur in the baths. Indeed, a few years later one witness observed that all kinds of people 'appeared so nakedly, and fearfully, in their uncouth naked postures' that he was reminded of the Resurrection.[12] In 1633, in order to keep order, the Corporation decreed that no one should enter the baths after 8 p.m. in the summer and 6 p.m. in winter. Failure to comply ensured a fine of 2s 6d. The guides – supposedly on hand to prevent disorder – were regularly dismissed for drunkenness.

By the time Fiennes and then Gale visited Bath, mixed bathing took place, but appropriate clothing was compulsory. In the Cross Bath women congregated on seats along the outer rim while the men swam or sat on the seats in the middle. Gale observed approvingly that 'with the greatest order and decency, the gentlemen keep to one side of the bath and the ladies the other'. If the seats were too low, cushions provided comfort, and hot wine boiled with sugar and herbs prevented bathers from fainting from the heat.[13] Gale noted that women took little basins into the water with them, tied to their arms with ribbons, in which to keep their handkerchiefs, nosegays and perfumes 'in case the exhalations of the water should be too prevalent'. Almost everyone, he observed, drank chocolate as they bathed.[14] Bathers could also receive beauty treatments in the water. The Dutch artist Willem Schellinks observed that a foot specialist removed bathers' corns and warts, and cut their nails.[15] Samuel Pepys, who visited Bath in 1668, cannot have been alone in his sentiment that 'methinks it cannot be clean to have so many bodies together in the same water'.[16]

Indeed, such personal grooming, as well as the treating of skin complaints, posed certain problems for spa-goers. Submerging infected sores or peeling skin in a communal bath clearly risked contaminating the waters and, therefore, infecting other bathers. A 1542 report noted that the Cross Bath was 'much frequented of People diseased with Lepre, Pokkes, Scabbes and great Aches'.[17] Public bathing was certainly not for the faint of heart. Smollett complained in *An Essay on the External Use of Water* of the nauseating spectacle of the filth washed from the bodies of the bathers 'left sticking to the sides of the place'. He found the conditions completely unhygienic. 'Diseased persons of all ages, sexes, and conditions, are promiscuously admitted into an open Bath', he observed. He thought it bad enough that the 'fair sex' were compelled to bathe with complete strangers; worse still was the fact that these strangers could be 'tainted with infectious distempers'.[18] His irascible fictional character Matthew Bramble is understandably offended when, taking to the waters of Bath, he finds that 'the first object that saluted my eye, was a child full of scrophulous ulcers, carried in the arms of one of the guides, under the very noses of the bathers'.[19]

Satirists such as Smollett were only too eager to point out the insalubrious consequences of those with skin diseases immersing themselves in water. In 1737 James Roberts lamented in his poem 'The Diseases of Bath': 'Nameless Diseases join'd pollute the Stream, / And mix their foul Infections with its Steam.' Cooks covered in grease and chimney sweeps in soot left their 'smut' behind as they bathed alongside lepers and others with skin diseases 'whose pealing scales upon the surface swim'. Roberts complains that he emerges from the bath 'mad and poison'd', covered with scales and dirt, cursing 'that Jakes obscene, / Whence I come sullied out who enter'd clean'.[20]

Another satirical poem in 1766 conjured even more revolting possibilities. Christopher Anstey in his *New Bath Guide* suggested that

Effects of the Cheltenham Waters, or tis Necessary to quicken your Motions after the Second Glass, published by S.W. Fores, 1828.

the water drunk in the Pump Room was recycled from the baths in which the filthy and diseased disported themselves. He described the women taking to the water 'like so many Spaniels' with 'wading Gentlemen up to their Necks', encouraged by a 'skilful and learned Physician' who declined to 'venture his Carcase himself'. He then describes the scenario by which a maid, Tabby, cleans herself in the water: 'So while Tabby was washing her Rump, / The ladies kept drinking it out of a Pump.'[21] Matthew Bramble fears such contamination and therefore makes inquiries, having 'a long conversation with the Doctor, about the construction of the pump and the cistern', but reaches the disturbing conclusion that he cannot be sure 'that the patients in the Pump-room don't swallow the scourings of the bathers'.[22] The fears about the waters lingered, causing such disquiet that as late as 1819, for his *Walks through Bath*, Pierce Egan, like a latter-day Bramble, determined 'upon inquiry' that Anstey and Smollett had merely been joking.[23]

The sight of bathers splashing in the steaming waters was greeted with humour by various observers. In the 1720s John Macky claimed that the 'Smoake and Slime of the waters, the promiscuous Multitude of the people in the *Bath*, with nothing but their Heads and Hands above Water', made him think of Michelangelo's painting of the damned on the altar wall of the Sistine Chapel.[24] Thirty years later a poet mocked bathers in a poem:

> 'Twas a glorious Sight to behold the Fair Sex
>   All wading with Gentlemen up to their Necks,
>   And view them so prettily tumble and sprawl
>   In a great smoking Kettle as big as our Hall.[25]

Plenty of opportunities existed for bathers to tumble and sprawl. Celia Fiennes described how exiting the baths involved a perilous and slippery ascent up a set of steps submerged in water, followed by a quick costume change. 'When you go out of the bath', she recorded, 'you go within a doore that leads to steps which you ascend by degrees, that are in the water, then the doore is shut which shuts down into the water a good way, so you are in a private place.' Here the bather was required to ascend several more steps, then 'let your canvass drop off by degrees into the water, which your women guides takes off'. At this point the bather's maid flung over her head 'a garment of flannell made like a nightgown with great sleeves' while the guide yanked on the tail of the bathing costume as the bather climbed yet more steps. 'Your other garment drops off,' she writes, 'so you are wrapped up.'[26]

Changing out of the wet canvas and linen costume was essential. Smollett (who trained as a doctor) noted that bathers risked 'imminent hazard' to their lives because the 'grievous nature of that dress' endangered the constitution: canvas quickly became 'cold and clammy' and clung to the body 'with a most hazardous adhesion'.[27] Smollett backed Archibald Cleland, the assistant surgeon at the recently opened General Hospital, who offered to improve conditions for bathers by creating purpose-built, single-sex changing facilities.[28] It is unclear why the Corporation rejected his proposal.

Once out of their wet costumes, bathers were transported back to their lodgings by sedan chair. However, sedan chairs were not always the most efficient mode of transport. The narrow streets of Bath frequently became congested with a sedan-chair traffic jam that forced the bathers to sit and shiver until they could pass. In 1749, to solve the problem, Cleland designed a

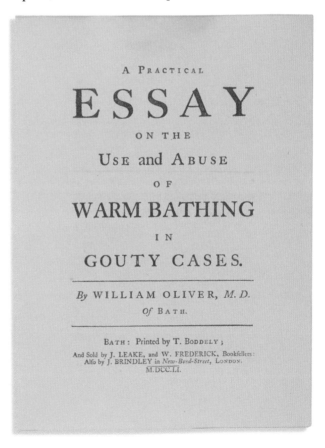

A PRACTICAL

ESSAY

ON THE

Use and Abuse

O F

WARM BATHING

I N

GOUTY CASES.

By WILLIAM OLIVER, *M.D.*

Of BATH.

BATH: Printed by T. BODDELY;
And Sold by J. LEAKE, and W. FREDERICK, Bookfellers:
Alfo by J. BRINDLEY in *New-Bond-Street*, LONDON.
M.DCC.LI.

Title page from *A Practical Essay on the Use and Abuse of Warm Bathing in Gouty Cases* by William Oliver, 1751.

new type of sedan chair, known as the 'Bath chair'. The new mode of transport was smaller than a general sedan, bellying out at the front and featuring an enclosed footstool at its base. Instead of a side window exposed to the elements, the Bath chair featured frames filled with starched linen, painted black on the outside and carried on short poles. One guide to the city described it as 'little black Box just the Size of a Coffin',[29] but this small size gave it a greater manoeuvrability in the sedan-chair crush of the streets as bathers were transported back to their lodgings.

THE DISEASE OF KINGS

Among those who received the greatest benefit from immersing themselves in the waters of Bath were sufferers from gout and various paralytic conditions. Daniel Defoe described seeing crutches in Bath, hung 'as the thank-offerings of those who have come hither lame, and gone away cur'd' – rather as Catholics left crutches and ex-votos at the shrines of saints.[30]

Gout was (and still is) a common complaint. Hippocrates called it 'the unwalkable disease', maintaining that it was an affliction of the rich and blaming it on too much wine, food and sex.[31] Indeed, gout was long viewed as a disease of the upper classes; it was known, thanks to famous sufferers such as Henry VIII and Philip II of Spain, as the 'disease of kings'. Attacks of gout are certainly exacerbated by certain foods – red meats, seafood, liver – of the sort enjoyed in the past by the wealthy. But gout affected all members of society, in part due to something they unwittingly consumed. The long-term accumulation of lead in the body has been shown to be associated with an increased level of uric acid.[32] Certain professions were particularly at risk from lead toxicity, such as plumbers, potters and painters, but most wines, and even Somerset ciders, were contaminated with lead from their containers or presses. Also, lead derivatives found in many everyday objects, such as pewter mugs, cooking utensils, cisterns and water pipes, ensured that doses of lead were virtually impossible to avoid. Women painted their face with lead, painters used it in their pigments, and food was coloured with lead chromate. Doctors even recommended lead to treat various conditions, such as dropsy diarrhoea, colic and – ironically – gout.

Dr William Buchan, in his 1769 bestseller, *Domestic Medicine: or, a Treatise on the Prevention and Cure of Diseases by Regimen and Simple Medicines*, frankly admitted that medicine was powerless before the gout. He recommended following a strict diet supplemented with a teaspoon of 'volatile liquor of hartshorn' (distilled deer horn) and the 'volatile tincture of guaiacum' (a plant used as a cure for syphilis).[33] Various other treatments had been recommended over the years, including one from 1518 that involved roasting a 'fat old goose' that had been stuffed with lard, incense, wax, rye flour and – alarmingly – kittens. In his *Complete Herbal* (1653), Nicolas Culpeper advised applying horseradish to the affected parts.[34]

The spa waters of Harrogate, Scarborough and Buxton were all recommended for relieving the symptoms of gout, but Bath proved the most effective. Physicians observed that patients' symptoms were eased, and in some cases cured, when bathing at Bath. In 1697 Robert Pierce published *Bath Memoirs, or, Observations in three and forty years practice at the Bath*, listing evidence of various patients cured of 'wandering scorbutical gout, wandering arthritick pains, fix'd pains, sciatica or hip gout'.[35] Pierce was no stranger to illness himself, having survived dropsy, smallpox, measles, malaria and tertian ague (despite all of which he lived into his eighty-eighth year). His treatise offered a number of case studies, such as that of the wife of the town clerk of Devizes, who was 'greatly afflicted with this wand'ring scorbutical gout', as well as with gravel and kidney stones. She had no wish to drink the waters, 'having some aversion to them', but quaffed a mixture of anti-arthritics and anti-scorbutics as she bathed. She improved after a week of this treatment, which continued for a month and eventually left her virtually gout-free. Pierce also cured his father-in-law, who, relieved of his crippling gout by paddling in both the King's Bath and the Cross Bath, left his crutches behind as a trophy.[36]

The waters of Bath probably were successful in treating other symptoms of lead contamination, in particular, weak and palsied limbs. Besides causing gout, lead pipes, pewter tankards and lead-glazed earthenware dishes also led to many cases of lead poisoning – a common but largely undiagnosed condition. The primary symptoms were fatigue, headaches, abdominal pain, constipation and, most seriously, severe weakness and paralysis of the limbs. As early as 1728 a doctor in Bath wrote to a friend, a physician in London, describing the positive effects of a visit to Bath on 'the great crop of Paralytics' – among them people working with lead such as colour grinders and pewterers – who arrived in the city for treatment. 'The palsies of such tradesmen', he noted, 'never fail of a cure by Bathing.'[37]

Recent scientific evidence shows that the optimism of these early doctors regarding the curative properties of the waters of Bath waters was well founded. In 1990 Audrey Heywood, a researcher at Southmead Hospital in Bristol, described how drinking and bathing in the spa waters of Bath could have cured eighteenth-century patients of lead poisoning.[38] Patients were immersed in water up to their necks, often in the Cross Bath, which was kept cooler than the others at a temperature of 35°C. Coincidentally, in the 1970s NASA scientists began preparing astronauts for the effects of weightlessness by immersing them up to their necks in water likewise heated to 35°C. The result was that the astronauts excreted high amounts of calcium through their urine. Since human bodies handle calcium and lead in a similar way, Heywood's team in the Immersion Laboratory in the Bristol Royal Infirmary began studying urinary lead excretion – and discovered that it was indeed increased during full-body immersion.

An 1813 depiction of the spa at Scarborough showing a dipper woman at work, *The Spa*, published by R. Ackermann.

Heywood also pointed out that Bath spa water is high in calcium – 390 milligrams per litre – as well as iron, and that scientific studies have shown that deficiencies in both can lead to a higher absorption of lead. One American report, she notes, suggests giving calcium and iron supplements to children who have raised levels of lead in their blood – the equivalent, in other words, of a glass or two of spa water from the Pump Room in Bath.

The waters of Bath *are* also sulphurous, with a sulphate content of 1015 mg/litre. The presence of H_2S is one of the main reasons for their therapeutic effect. Acute exposures to H_2S is dangerous and even life-threatening. However, bathing in mineral waters, where the H_2S is slowly absorbed through a topical application in a well-ventilated setting, possesses numerous beneficial effects.

Many recent studies have shown that sulphur baths can be used successfully to treat skin diseases such as dermatitis and psoriasis, respiratory problem such as chronic obstructive pulmonary disease, and even, in athletes, exercise-induced muscle damage. Sulphurous mineral water possesses anti-inflammatory and antioxidant properties that can also help in the managing of chronic pain and disorders such as arthritis and peripheral nerve injury. Used in a clinical environment (as opposed to a spa) it can alleviate conditions such as arterial hypertension, atherosclerosis, heart failure, peptic ulcer, Parkinson's, Alzheimer's, and even erectile dysfunction.[39]

DRINKING THE WATERS

By the middle of the eighteenth century, more people drank the waters of Bath than bathed in them. In the 1720s Daniel Defoe wrote of Bath that 'the medicinal virtue of these waters had been useful to the diseased people by bathing in them, now they are found to be useful also, taken into the body; and there are many more come to drink the waters, than to bathe in them.'[40] Defoe claimed the practice of drinking the waters at Bath was some fifty years old, and indeed the town's waters only became safe and popular to drink after 1650, when a fresh supply was piped directly from a spring. Soon quaffing water in the Pump Room came to be a more popular activity in Bath than immersing oneself in the waters. This change was lamented in 1739 by David Kinneir, who believed that bathing was falling from favour because fine ladies feared it might disturb their elaborate coiffures.[41] Another reason is given in Fanny Burney's 1778 novel *Evelina*, where one of the characters, Mr Lovel, watching the women bathers from the Pump Room, declares it 'very incomprehensible why the ladies choose that frightful unbecoming dress to bathe in!' To which a female character replies: 'I always hated bathing, because one can get no pretty dress for it.'[42] Tellingly, neither Evelina nor her companions takes to the waters.

Bathing became increasingly unpopular with the beau monde, and by the early years of the 1800s the public baths were used almost exclusively by the sick and the poor – or, as an 1803 guide put it, 'by hospital invalids or by persons of the lower class of life ... little regarded by people of condition'.[43]

Drinking the waters was another matter. Dr Buchan provided information on how, when and how much mineral water to take, and when not to take it. The best months for drinking spa water, he claimed, were April, May and June, as well as August, September and October, with the course continuing for six weeks. He advised that patients suffering from fevers and ulcerations (especially pulmonary and intestinal) should avoid drinking spa water. Patients drinking the water for the first time were to ensure that they had performed 'proper previous evacuations' – thanks to an emetic (to induce vomiting) and a timely visit to the chamber pot. In some cases, especially in those of a sanguine temperament, he advised that 'bleeding may be proper'. The water was to be consumed on an empty stomach, an hour before a meal, with the first and largest dose taken before breakfast, the second before dinner (the noon meal), and then the smallest dose before supper.[44]

Some waters, such as those at Spa in Belgium, were said by one author, writing in 1734, to have 'a delightful flavour'.[45] But most tasted foul, and the experience of Jeremy Melford at Harrogate, described in Tobias Smollett's 1771 novel *The Expedition of Humphry Clinker*, may not have been atypical. He claimed that one drink of these healing waters 'cured me of all desire to repeat the medicine'. Some said it smelled like rotten eggs, he wrote, others like 'the scourings of a foul gun', while to Jeremy 'it is exactly that of bilge-water'. He claimed that to down the liquid he was obliged to hold his nose with one hand, while afterwards he felt 'sickness, griping, and insurmountable disgust. I can hardly mention it without puking.'[46] An even more unpleasant experience awaited those who drank the waters from the well at Acton, near London. A 1760 treatise described it as 'moderately bitter and somewhat of a nauseous Taste', but the real challenge came afterwards: it was one of the 'strongest purging Waters near London', and was therefore noted for causing 'a great Soreness' in the anus.[47]

Unsurprisingly, a little assistance was sometimes required to make drinking spa water palatable. To disguise the vileness of Latham's spa water, the Dutch wife of the 8th Earl of Derby, Dorothea Helena, set up a small enterprise supplying additives to enhance its flavour. Her flavourings included coriander seeds and angelica roots (wild celery), as well as lemon and orange. At Bristol Hotwells, the physician Tobias Venner recommended disguising the salty taste by adding sugar, honey, cream of tartar and a tincture of violets or roses. However, Dr Buchan claimed the waters in Bristol were 'agreeable to the taste'. He noted that the water was 'usually mingled with wine, but is much better unmixed'.[48]

Buchan advised patients to start off with 'a small dose ... a wine-glass or two, twice or thrice in the forenoon'. The dose could then be raised as the days passed, with those in the Pump Room at Bath advised to treat themselves, when their constitution allowed, to a total of two quarts per day.[49] He pointed out that at first the water had a tendency to raise the pulse rate slightly, increase the heat of the body and induce drowsiness, 'but these effects soon disappear'. The first few doses might induce 'costiveness' – that is, constipation – but this condition, too, disappeared soon enough. The waters first exerted their 'stimulating properties' on the stomach, exciting 'a pleasing glow in this organ'. This glow was succeeded by an increase in appetite, a lifting of the spirits and 'a quick determination to the kidneys'. (Back to the chamber pot to make water.) He noted that a constellation of unpleasant symptoms, such as headache, thirst, a dry tongue or giddiness, meant the treatment should be discontinued.

Immediately after drinking the water, patients were to 'use moderate exercise', and during the entire six-week period a careful diet and regular hours should be observed, 'and the mind should be kept in as tranquil a state as possible'.[50]

The happy effects of drinking spa water are described in a poem, 'A Trip to Tunbridge', published in 1719:

I began with one Glass, and soon got to five,
Which made me so perfectly fresh and alive,
That I danc'd, sung and raffled, drank Coffee and Tea,
And from Morning to Night was as brisk as a Bee.[51]

The poet fails to mention the purgative effect of drinking the water, and his possibly urgent visit to the privy. It was appropriate that many writers spoke of spring waters coming from 'the bowels of the earth', for bowels, quite literal ones, received much attention in places such as Bath and Tunbridge Wells.[52] In 1753, while attending her friend William Pitt the Elder at Tunbridge Wells, Elizabeth Montagu fretted that the physicians had been neglecting his insomnia and low spirits while 'giving all their attention to the disorder in his bowels'.[53] Christopher Anstey's *New Bath Guide* described the bowel-obsessed physician visited by the narrator on his arrival in Bath – a doctor who 'talked of the peritoneum and colon' as well as of 'foeculent matter that swells the abdomen'. The consultation finishes with a definitive assessment: 'But the noise I have heard in my bowels, like thunder, / Is a flatus, I find, in my left hypochonder.'[54]

PASSING WATER

The hypochonder was not the only part of the anatomy to get a workout from a glass or two of spa water; the bladder was equally engaged. 'I hope, Madam, you piss well': such was the salutation that a man in Tunbridge Wells addressed to a female friend in

London. He explained that the 'chiefest complement' among women was: 'I hope the waters pass well with your ladyship.'[55]

Difficulty in micturition – problems passing urine – was a common complaint, often caused by kidney and bladder stones. Drinking spa waters such as those in Tunbridge Wells was said to enable the patient able to 'pass water' by aiding in the decomposition of these stones. In 1792 the aptly named John Leake wrote a medical treatise, arguing in his chapter on 'Diseases of the Kidney, Bladder and Urine' that drinking spa waters in spas such as Knaresborough assisted with the passage of urine.[56]

Another spa water was likewise reported to be sovereign for micturition – that from Holt in Leicestershire, known (after the proprietor, Cosmo Nevil) as Nevil-Holt Spaw-Water. The author of a 1749 treatise on its virtues cited the case of a 'married woman, of a thin, scrofulous habit' who, after the birth of her child, 'laboured under extream difficulty of making water for six weeks'. After a month of drinking a daily pint of Nevil-Holt Spaw-Water, 'the difficulty and heat of making urine' disappeared, and she became 'healthy and florid'.[57] The author was helpful enough to point out that bottles of this special mineral water were available in London from Mr Jones at the Wheat Sheaf in Tavistock Street in Covent Garden and from Mr Thomas Proctor at the Golden Key in the piazza in front of the Royal Exchange.

Spas obviously needed to make provisions for those who, soon after consuming the water, needed to answer the call of nature. Often these facilities were of the most basic sort. In 1670 Latham Spa in Lancashire, owned by Charles Stanley, 8th Earl of Derby, publicized that visitors could relieve themselves in a private spot – behind bushes in an adjacent field. When Lady Elmes visited Astrop Spa in Northamptonshire in 1665, she complained about the primitive conditions. No shelter offered visitors respite from inclement weather when drinking at the well or when relieving themselves afterwards.

Seventy-five years later, patrons to the same spa hardly enjoyed a superior experience. A new building did cover the well, and refreshments were served, but to relieve themselves visitors were obliged to retreat behind a 12-foot-high hedge. When the haughty Sarah Churchill, Duchess of Marlborough, visited Scarborough Spa in 1732 she was appalled by the facilities or lack thereof – for she discovered that, once the waters went to work, the women were expected to relieve themselves in clear view of one another, 'above 20 holes with drawers under them to take out'. A pile of leaves was thoughtfully provided, 'which the ladies take in with them'.[58]

The more well-established spas of the Continent were little better. A 1764 guide to German spas noted that the process of elimination offered 'some little inconveniences, or embarrassments, especially to the ladies', who needed to seek out 'a commodious place behind some large stone'.[59] Even the facilities in Bath following the arrival of Beau Nash left much to be desired. Daniel Defoe complained that the town 'scarce gives the company room to converse out of the smell of their own excrements'.[60]

BOTTLING IT

Nevil-Holt Spaw-Water was only one of many brands of bottled waters available in London and other English cities and towns. Waters from Continental spas, such as Seltzer and Spa, could be purchased in shops. The tea and coffee merchant Thomas Twining imported 7,000 bottles of water from Spa in 1721; he also sold water from Bath and Epsom.[61] The bestselling physician Dr William Buchan pointed out that spa water travelled and kept well so long as – like a good bottle of wine – it was well corked.[62] Sarah Churchill may not have rated Scarborough, which she found primitive and ugly, but its waters did her such good during her 1732 visit that she bottled some to take back home with her, corking jars that she sealed with wax for the long carriage ride.

The ability to drink spa waters at home possessed an obvious appeal, doing away with the need for a possibly expensive journey to one of the wells: one could simply 'take the waters' at home. In 1754 Robert Whytt, a professor of medicine in Edinburgh, experimented with concocting an artificial spa water, 'lime-water', made from mixing water with quicklime. He also experimented with making a medicinal water from powdered oyster shells, which he assured his colleagues 'were got from among the rubbish on the south side of the Castle of Edinbrugh and were quite free of any sea-salt'.[63]

THE
Medicinal VIRTUES
OF
TAR WATER
FULLY EXPLAINED,
BY THE
Right Rev. Dr. GEORGE BERKELEY,
Lord Bifhop of CLOYNE, in *Ireland.*
To which is ADDED,
The RECEIPT for making it, and Inftructions to
know by the Colour and Tafte of the Water
when the *TAR* is good, and of the right Sort.
TOGETHER WITH
A plain Explanation of the BISHOP's *Phy-
fical* Terms.
*Defigned for the Benefit of all who drink it, and thofe
who make it themfelves.*

5.

DUBLIN Printed.
LONDON Reprinted, for the Proprietors of the
TAR-WATER Warehoufe, behind the *Thatch'd-
Houfe-Tavern,* in St. *James's-Street* ; and Sold
by *M. Cooper* in *Pater-nofter-row.* 1744.
[Price Six-pence.]

George Berkeley, *The Medical Virtues of Tar Water*, a pamphlet from 1744.

The greatest success in concocting a medicinal water to be consumed at home was the tar-water invented by the Irish philosopher and divine George Berkeley, Bishop of Cloyne. Berkeley was concerned about how to combat the epidemics that struck Ireland in 1741, and more generally how to improve the daily lives of the people, especially the poor. Having successfully treated his own family with this concoction, which he distilled from pine resin, he decided to spread the word of its virtues. To that end, in 1744 he published *Siris: A Chain of Philosophical Reflexions and Inquiries concerning the Virtues of Tar Water*. He believed his drink to be sovereign for all manner of ailments. 'I freely own', he declared, 'that I suspect tar-water is a panacea … a Medicine that cures or relieves all the different Species of Distempers.'[64] The work quickly became a bestseller, with Princess Caroline trying the drink and the novelist Horace Walpole writing that 'we are now mad about tar-water'.[65] Before 1744 was out, the Tar-Water Warehouse had opened in St James's Street in London, *Siris* had run through six editions, and popular ballads were singing Berkeley's praises. Physicians remained sceptical. James Jurin, later president of the Royal College of Physicians, summed up his damning critique of Berkeley's panacea: 'As Bishop of Cloyne, I honour and respect [you], but as a Physician, I despise and pity You.'[66] However, tar-water remained around long enough for Uncle Pumblechook to discover it diluting his brandy in Dickens's *Great Expectations*, published almost 120 years after tar-war mania gripped the nation.

GREEN SICKNESS

If bathing in waters proved beneficial for certain conditions such as gout and lead poisoning, so too drinking the waters treated various afflictions. One of the most notable was green sickness, an ailment in which the patient, always a young woman, presented with poor colour, palpitations, headache, drowsiness, swollen ankles and eyelids, and – most revealingly – 'a suppression of the menstrual discharge'.[67] A seventeenth- or eighteenth-century physician would quickly make the diagnosis of green sickness, otherwise known as the 'disease of virgins'. More often than not, a trip to a spa would be prescribed.

The reference to the colour green is a bit of a mystery, since medical practitioners rarely referred to a greenish complexion in sufferers; it may have been a reference, instead, to the youth of the patients, always young girls of marriageable age. Also known less colloquially as chlorosis, a term first used in 1619, green sickness was caused (we now know) by low haemoglobin levels typical of hypochromic anaemia. But in the seventeenth and eighteenth centuries it was believed to be caused when a blockage – 'obstructions of veins about the womb' – prevented menstruation.[68] The trapped blood therefore migrated upwards, affecting the heart and causing various mental disturbances that, at the least, caused 'frequent sighing without knowing the cause'[69] and, in the worst cases, could result in suicide. Quacks prescribed numerous elixirs to treat the condition, but one of the most reliable treatments was, apparently, marriage – 'for when they become pregnant', one medical text declared, 'they will be cured'.[70]

A less drastic (and, no doubt, more effective) remedy for green sickness was for the patient to visit a spa. Tunbridge Wells was supposedly particularly effective, since its waters, according to a 1714 treatise, 'very often cure the Greensickness in Maids'.[71] Dr Buchan agreed, writing that the medicinal waters of Tunbridge Wells were good for treating 'those feverish exacerbations occasioned by the green-sickness'.[72] Buchan believed that those most susceptible to the conditions were girls of 'a lazy, indolent disposition', and so he recommended exertions in the open air – such as, perhaps, one found in a spa such as Tunbridge Wells.

Drinking the waters at Tunbridge Wells, or waters from another chalybeate spring, would in fact have been an advisable remedy for someone suffering from chlorosis, whose link to iron deficiency was recognized in the 1930s. Drinking chalybeate mineral waters — that is, those impregnated with iron — treated anaemia, so a trip to the spa no doubt helped many young women. Besides Tunbridge Wells, notable chalybeate springs were found in Cheltenham, Harrogate, Hove, Monkswell in Lincolnshire, and Scarborough. As early as 1670 young women with green sickness were encouraged to drink three quarts of Scarborough's spring water a day.[73] Such a liquid diet would have ensured that, besides having their chlorosis treated, they would also piss well.

FIVE

'All the amusements'

A SEASON IN BATH

'O Molly!' writes the servant Winnifred Jenkins in Tobias Smollett's 1771 novel *The Expedition of Humphry Clinker*, 'you that live in the country have no deception of our doings at Bath. Here is such dressing, and fidling, and dancing, and gadding, and courting and plotting – O gracious! if God had not given me a good stock of discretion, what a power of things might not I reveal.'[1]

Dressing, music, dancing, gossiping and plotting, gadding about – such things did indeed make up the routine for many visitors to Bath. The poet Alexander Pope wrote during a visit in 1714: 'I have Slid, I cannot tell how, into all the Amusements of this place: My whole Day is shared by the Pump-assemblies, the Walkes, the chocolate houses, Raffling Shops, Plays Medleys.'[2]

Pope did admit that, in the midst of all this socializing, he was also taking the waters, and moreover that they did him good. The naturally hot waters of Bath were nominally the greatest attraction for visitors – the reason for making the long journey over the rough roads. But after having gone for an early-morning bath, then to the Pump Room for a flask or two of purgative water, a visitor to Bath would be ready for a daily campaign of entertainments.

'A modern belle going to the rooms at Bath' by James Gillray. This hand-coloured etching from 1796 shows a fashionable young lady with a comically large plume in her hat.

Even before the arrival of Beau Nash, Bath was said to be 'more famed for pleasure than for cures'.[3] When Daniel Defoe visited in the 1720s, during the height of Nash's reign, he noted that the city was 'the resort of the sound, rather than the sick'.[4] He said the same of Tunbridge Wells – that 'company and diversion is in short the main business of the place'.[5] Indeed, these spas held attractions for those other than merely martyrs to gout, dropsy and scrofulous skin diseases. As John Wilmot, the Earl of Rochester, wrote regarding Bath, pilgrims arrived 'for Ease, Disease, for Lechery and Sport'.[6]

Bath featured many coffee houses, where, for a penny, men of any social standing could mix and mingle, enjoying lively conversation. Men often breakfasted here following their early-morning bath and then their glasses of thermal water in the Pump Room. Coffee houses in spa resorts, for obvious reasons, attracted a particular type of clientele. 'I could not help contemplating the company, with equal surprise and compassion', Smollett's Matthew Bramble observed when he visited a coffee house in Bath.

> We consisted of thirteen individuals; seven lamed by the gout, rheumatism, or palsy; three maimed by accident; and the rest either deaf or blind. One hobbled, another hopped, a third dragged his legs after him like a wounded snake, a fourth straddled betwixt a pair of long crutches, like the mummy of a felon hanging in chains; a fifth was bent into a horizontal position, like a mounted telescope, shoved in by a couple of chairmen; and a sixth was the bust of a man, set upright in a wheel machine, which the waiter moved from place to place.[7]

Spa-goers might attend a church service following their exertions in the water (the one at Bath Abbey commenced at 11 a.m.). But many other excursions were available in Bath: promenading in the latest fashions, horseback riding, trotting around in a horse-drawn carriage, taking a stroll in one of the pleasure gardens or browsing

Milsom Street, Bath, a 1784 watercolour by Thomas Malton. This street became famous for its exclusive shops

around the latest shops. Clothing shops were naturally in great demand. Indeed, what differentiated a spa resort from an ordinary city or town was its abundance of luxury shops. The French author Abbé Prévost described shops in English spa towns as 'dealers in all kinds of jewels, delicacies, and gallantries'. They take 'advantage of a kind of enchantment which blinds everyone in these realms of enjoyment, to sell for their weight in gold trifles one is ashamed of having bought after leaving the place'.[8]

Small wooden box, inlaid with naturally coloured wood veneers (Tunbridgeware), inset with a pincushion, made in Tunbridge Wells by T. Barton, 1800–1840.

Such was the demand for high fashion in Bath that haberdashers, hairdressers, hatters and hosiers arrived for the season from London. Elizabeth Montagu described how even elderly ladies visiting Bath dressed to attract attention: 'They wear on their heads a thing called a caleche, which makes them look like the hooded serpent preserved in museums', she wrote to one of her friends. 'A friseur [hairdresser] is employed three hours in a morning to make a young lady look like a Virgin Hottentot or Squaw, all art ends in giving them the ferocious air of uncombed savages.'[9] The fashion for tall, feathered headdresses and wigs made travel in sedan chairs problematic. The Bath Chairmen's Petition, comically printed in the *Bath Chronicle*, announced that, despite their attempts to make women 'sit easy', their task was made difficult because 'your heads are grown double the length of your waist'.[10]

Many other luxury items besides clothes and hats could be purchased. 'One can step out of doors and get a thing in five minutes', gushes Mrs Allen in Jane Austen's *Northanger Abbey*.[11] Bath was famous for selling extravagant knick-knacks and disseminating the latest fads from London or Paris. Josiah Wedgwood, whose wife required treatment in Bath, opened showrooms in the Westgate Buildings in 1772 before moving to Milsom Street two years later. He grudgingly allowed that 'there are tolerably decent shops enow here already'.[12] Indeed there were. Many shops sold what were known as 'toys', which in the eighteenth century meant playthings for adults – watches, snuffboxes, porcelain, pretty baubles – rather than for children. Each toy shop was unique, such as that of George Speren, whose premises in Orange Grove only sold fans featuring scenes of Bath, or Mrs Bertram's shop, which Lady Mary Wortley Montagu described as 'the warehouse of the fop' that sold 'deluding traps to girls and boys'.[13] Mrs Bertram's sister Mary Chenevix operated a similar shop in Tunbridge Wells. Many proprietors were also craftsmen such as goldsmiths, jewellers and watchmakers who operated small workshops from the back of their shops. One of the most famous was the one on Milsom Street owned by brothers George and John Evill. It featured musical clocks, toiletry sets, spectacles and firearms with engraved filigree. For a small fee they even hired out silver cutlery and candlesticks to visitors.

It was from this shop that in 1771 Richard Brinsley Sheridan purchased many items, including such necessities as a toothpick case, a hair locket, a ring and two seals, a picture in a case, a pair of garnet buttons and a pair of swords and foils. Sheridan may have felt ashamed for having bought such trifles, as the Abbé Prévost claimed, but at least the sword came in handy: he later used it in two duels with Captain Thomas Matthews, defending the honour of his wife,

Vase made of Blue John, c.1860–85. Blue John is the name given to the purple-blue fluorspar found only in Treak Cliff, near Castleton in Derbyshire. It was worked into ornaments and jewellery sold at Buxton spa.

singer Eliza Linley — a soprano whose career began in Bath when she was 9 years old.

Other spas also sold expensive finery to their visitors. Tunbridge Wells featured Tunbridge Ware, an intricate inlaid woodwork that decorated boxes, tea chests, paperweights, cribbage boards and snuff boxes.[14] Buxton produced furniture and gifts similar to Tunbridge Ware but using a dark limestone instead of wood. The polished black stone was inlaid with semi-precious stones and minerals elaborately shaped into flowers or patterns. It was also possible to buy jewellery or ornaments in Buxton made from a local stone, Blue John, found in the rock of Castleton in Derbyshire.[15] And in Bristol Hotwells jewellery adorned with Bristol diamonds, a quartz crystal found in the Avon Gorge, was in high demand.

Naturally one ate and drank well in spas such as Bath and Tunbridge Wells. Visitors could enjoy expensive wines, Essex oysters, fish from Brixham, Welsh butter, Yorkshire hams, and even the newest flavours in syllabubs — a frothy drink made from alcohol and whipped cream. The first ice-cream parlour in Bath, the brainchild of Benjamin Forde, opened on Pulteney Bridge in 1774, advertising ice creams made from the 'best sweetmeats, essences and fruits', which could be ordered for house parties and sold at 4d a glass. Forde also sold an almond drink, orgeat, as well as lemonade, and cakes and Italian biscuits 'decorated elegantly'.[16] Some shops ran takeaway services, offering hot stews, tarts, pies, soups or spit-roasted meats, tarts and pies. International foods were on offer. Thomas Wiltshire sold exotic fare inspired by West Indian cuisine, such as spicy turtles. The Shum brothers in Cheap Street, and John Peterswald near Trim Bridge, offered German and Italian sausages. Edmund Rack, founder of the Bath and West of England Society, wrote in his journal in 1780 that the latest table delicacy in Bath was chickens fed on chopped almonds and raisins and sold at 2 guineas a brace. 'The Pastry Cooks who

'Gouty Gourmands at Dinner', in Thomas Rowlandson's satirical 1798 collection *The Comforts of Bath.*

have introduced this will get fortunes, as many are sold daily at that price.'[17]

One of the most famous bakers in Bath in the eighteenth century was William Dalmer. Not only did he produce Bath Oliver biscuits, but he inherited the recipe of Sally Lunns – the brioche-like buns that first appeared in Bath in the late seventeenth century thanks to a (possibly fictional) Huguenot refugee named Solange Luyon. Dalmer baked them in a portable oven and distributed them throughout the city. In 1799 he claimed in the *Bath Chronicle* that it was 'light and easy of digestion, keeps remarkably moist, and ... exceed[s] in quality and quantity any Bread in the city'. He offered delivery to anywhere in the city. In the same advertisement, Dalmer made the extraordinary admission that one of his delivery boys attempted to set fire to one of his barrows in the Circus, and that a financial reward of 1 guinea was on offer for the capture of the culprit.[18]

English spa towns could also offer visitors curiosities and other more intellectual fare. By the middle of the eighteenth century Bath had bookshops in Terrace Walk, Orange Grove and Wade's Passage. Leamington Spa featured 'Bisset's Museum of Natural History and Grand Cabinet of Curiosities', which could be visited for a shilling. James Bisset opened his museum in his home in 1812, displaying an African royal throne, a Turkish dagger and a Chinese shield, as well as birds' eggs and stuffed animals.

Bisset did much to promote his adopted town of Leamington Spa, extolling it in verse and establishing a library. Visitors to other spa towns could likewise enjoy the benefits of circulating libraries, such as Morley's library in Tunbridge Wells (for which a subscription cost 2 shillings and sixpence), Bott's in Buxton, and the one in Cheltenham, which, as Simeon Moreau boasted, 'besides the usual assortment of novels, &c. contains as select a collection of valuable books as may be found in many of greater extent, and much more noted, at other water-drinking places'.[19] Not only that, but subscribers could borrow harpsichords, pianofortes and other musical instruments. In Bath, Marshall's Circulating Library, situated at the top of Milsom Street, encompassed an impressive 20,000 volumes. For 15 shillings a year or 5 shillings a quarter, guests could borrow books, reassured that the proprietor is 'daily adding every NEW BOOK in the *English*, *French*, and *Italian* Languages, together with all the New Pamphlets, Magazine, Reviews, &c. as soon as published'.[20] In the 1790s subscribers to Marshall's supposedly included two princes, five dukes, four duchesses, seven earls, fourteen countesses and forty-three knights of the realm.

These libraries and their purpose-built reading rooms featured Bibles and the Book of Common Prayer, as well as newspapers from London, Edinburgh and Dublin. Such establishments also acted as

'Circulating Library', in *Poetical Sketches of Scarborough*, published by R. Ackermann with plates by Thomas Rowlandson, 1813.

news centres and registries for lodgings and servants. Newspapers could also be read in coffee houses. In Cheltenham a coffee house opened in one of the local taverns, The Plough, which each morning received all the London newspapers. The Little Fanmaker in Bath, a tea and china shop owned by Thomas Loggon, permitted clients to read the *Bath Journal* as well as other papers for 2 shillings and sixpence a season. Loggon was quite literally a little fanmaker – a man of short stature who painted ladies' fans.

Bookshops were also venues in which to exchange news and gossip as well as to acquire books. The London bookseller and printer James Leake took over his father-in-law's bookshop in Bath in 1723. Leake sold books and, for a fee, loaned them out. Mary Chandler's *Description of Bath*, printed by Leake in 1734, described his establishment as a 'safe Retreat' whose 'bending Shelves' were thronged with 'Heroes of antient, and of modern Song'.[21] However, a writer and lawyer named Matthew Concanen, who wrote under the pen name Thomas Goulding, claimed to be less impressed with Leake's bookshop. His satirical *Essay Against too Much Reading*, printed in 1728, argued that excessive reading was detrimental to health, undoing all the good of 'taking the waters'. Reading was responsible, he maintained, for deformities such as 'swell'd Legs, broad at Hips like the Dutch, Short-back'd, Round-shoulder'd, Short-neck'd, flat at Chest, and staring Eyes'.[22]

A NIGHT ON THE TILES

Thanks to the entrepreneurial flair of Beau Nash, dancing at balls was one of the highlights of 'taking the waters'. He introduced two dances a week at Bath, on Tuesdays and Wednesdays. They commenced at 6 p.m. and finished, on the dot, at 11 p.m. Attendance was by subscription only, paid in advance.

Balls always opened with minuets, a dance for two imported from France that consisted of small steps (the word 'minuet' comes from the Latin *minutus*, 'small' or 'minute'). The very word 'minuet' apparently caused trepidation in many young women. 'How many fine Women do we see totter with Fear, when they are taken out to dance?' Philip Thicknesse asked.[23] These nerves can be understood, since only one couple was permitted to dance on the floor at one time, with the entire company, sitting on benches, silently watching them. The young lady was escorted to her seat once her dance finished, at which point the Master of Ceremonies guided another young lady to the gentleman, who remained on the floor. When this second dance was over, the couple returned to their seats while the Master of Ceremonies escorted another pair to the floor, and the whole process began again. Each man therefore danced with two ladies, with the Master of Ceremonies plotting the order of the dancing and who should dance with whom. Matthew Bramble, the crusty protagonist of Smollett's *Humphry Clinker*, claimed to find the spectacle 'a tiresome repetition of the same languid, frivolous scene, performed by actors that seemed to sleep in all their motions'. The performances were, he maintained, devoid of all 'beauty, grace, activity, magnificent dress, or a variety of any kind'.[24]

These minuets persisted for two hours until precisely 8 p.m. At that point the benches were removed, signalling that English, Scottish and Irish country dancing was about to commence. Bramble likewise failed to enjoy these frolics. 'The most violent stinks, and the most powerful perfumes contended for the mastery', he claimed.

> Imagine to yourself a high exalted essence of mingled odours, arising from putrid gums, imposthumated lungs, sour flatulencies, rank arm-pits, sweating feet, running sores and issues, plasters, ointments, and embrocations, hungary-water, spirit of lavender, assa-foetida drops, musk, hartshorn, and sal volatile; besides a thousand frowzy steams, which I could not analyse.

He maintained that these 'pestilential vapours' and a 'compound of villainous smells' in the room made him feel quite faint.[25]

Those of higher rank were always first on the dance floor, chosen, of course, by the Master of Ceremonies. Dancing continued until the clock struck 9 p.m., when the company observed a short interval to catch the breath, drink a cup of tea and snack on treats. The dances commenced until the Master of Ceremonies snapped his fingers and ended the evening at the prescribed hour – the rigorously observed 11 p.m.

Country dancing eventually became so popular that the minuets gradually disappeared by the end of the eighteenth century. New dances were invented and given such names as 'Lady Coventry's Delight', 'The Chinese Festival', 'The Partridge', 'Trip to Bath', 'The Devil on Two Sticks' and 'Plum Pudding'. Another dance, a French country jig named the cotillion, was introduced to England

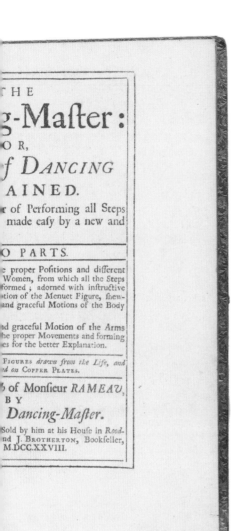

John Essex's popular *The Dancing-Master: or The Art of Dancing Explained*, published in 1728.

in 1766. By 1771 it had become popular in assembly rooms throughout England. A dance performed in squares by four sets of couples, its name came from the French word for petticoats — a reference to how the ladies flashed their petticoats, or undergarments, as they danced. Concerned moralists disapproved, fearing that it permitted too much physical contact between the sexes — which was precisely, of course, the reason for its popularity.

Dancing lessons were imperative if one hoped to perform well at a ball. Dance teachers gave instruction in the minuet, formal dances and country dancing; they also imparted social graces.

Perhaps the most famous dance teacher of the eighteenth century was John Essex. In 1728 he published *The Dancing Master*, which was full of illustrations and useful information on how to perform on the dance floor. He taught many other skills too, helping people to carry themselves gracefully. 'It is very necessary for everyone,' he pointed out, 'in what station of life soever he be, to know how to take off his Hat as he ought, and to make a handsome Bow.' Yet he noted that different occasions required different sorts of bow, and so he undertook to 'explain each in particular'. He spent many pages on how women should conduct themselves, for a woman who carried herself with her head upright and her body 'well disposed, without Affectation, or too much Boldness', would be treated as a 'stately Lady' – unlike those who carried themselves 'negligently', stooped, or poked their heads forward. Essex tells the reader that he aims to teach 'Youth the Manner of Behaviour in publick Places' and, by following his advice, 'those that assist at Balls, and those that make the Company, will distinguish themselves only by their good Manners and Breeding.'[26]

In the 1730s Francis Fleming and his wife became Bath's foremost dance instructors. Fleming continued, following his wife's death, visiting Paris each year to keep abreast of the latest dances. Fleming was also an accomplished musician, who conducted the Pump Room orchestra and then, after 1744, took charge of music in the Assembly Rooms. One of the members of his orchestra in the Pump Room was Thomas Chilcot, a composer and harpsichordist who also played the organ in Bath Abbey. One of Chilcot's pupils was Thomas Linley, a composer and concert master from Bath, later to become director of music at the Drury Lane Theatre in London. His beautiful and talented daughter Elizabeth, the soprano, married Sheridan. His son, Thomas Linley Jr, was a child prodigy known as the 'English Mozart', giving a solo violin concerto in Bath at the age of 8 in 1764. He met Mozart himself but, tragically, drowned in an accident at the age of 22. Mozart declared him a 'true genius' who 'would have been one of the greatest ornaments of the musical world'.[27]

It is a credit to the musical society of Bath, and an indication of its high quality, that young Linley's enormous talent – like that of Thomas Lawrence – had been nurtured in the city. Indeed, music had long been part of the experience at Bath, with Willem

Schellinks's 1662 sketch showing musicians playing on the steps of the King's Bath. Pepys was certainly impressed with the quality of music on his 1668 visit, noting that after being carried back from his bath he listened to music, 'extraordinary good as ever I heard in London'.[28] Music was important not merely for entertainment – it was regarded, like water, as part of the cure. Physicians in Bath urged Nash to implement an orchestra for the health of the visitors: 'The least stroke imaginable upon any music instrument', they wrote, 'has such an effect on the human body ... and consequently the spirits are not only raised, or made finer, but the other animal fluids are also briskly agitated.'[29] Nash duly obliged, hiring musicians from London and hosting them in the Pump Room. Likewise, Simeon Moreau, the Master of Ceremonies in Cheltenham, maintained that it was 'highly probable' that music, because it gave such delight, 'may contribute to the operation of the water with greater success'. As he explained: 'The spirits being put into motion, and most agreeably touched by the harmony of the instruments, the sensible fibres become more pliant, and the several organs better adapted to the free exercise of their different functions.'[30]

Not everyone, apparently, found the music therapeutic at first, for, as Lydia in Smollett's *Humphry Clinker* lamented, the 'noise of the music playing in the gallery' – a semicircular balcony added to the Pump Room in Bath in 1751 – together with the 'hum and buzz' of conversation contributed to headache and vertigo. However, she claimed that eventually these noises 'became familiar and even agreeable'. A worse fate befell the audience for a violinist named Ralph Thicknesse. In 1741 his performance of one of his own concertos in the Assembly Rooms was terminated when he collapsed and died. The doctors found he had succumbed to an attack of nerves, but his brother Philip blamed the waters he had drunk liberally in the Pump Room earlier that day.

If dancing was permitted on only two nights a week at Bath, spa-goers found themselves with five nights to find other ways to amuse themselves. Gaming and betting were, for many, an essential part of the week's entertainment. Indeed, the eighteenth century was addicted to gambling. No fashionable or elegant gathering was complete without card games such as Ace of Hearts, Basset, Hazard and Pharaoh or Faro, which were popular with both men and women. In 1713 a newspaper reporter claimed to obtain 'great pleasure' from seeing women gambling. 'Their natural tenderness is a weakness here easily unlearned, and I find my soul exalted when I see a lady sacrifice the fortune of her children with as little concern as a Spartan or a Roman dame.' Their avaricious faces were twisted, he noted, into 'violent distortions'.[31]

Gambling was the undoing of many in the eighteenth century – including Beau Nash himself. From a young age Nash had used gambling to finance his opulent lifestyle, and he became so notorious that a book about the tricks of professional gamblers, thieves and pickpockets, written in a Taunton prison by a convicted thief, John Poulter, was allegedly dedicated to him.[32] The dedication may have been unfair, but a cloud did hover over Nash because of a new card game known as E.O. (even and odd). This game developed after gambling became such a problem in Britain that Gaming Acts were passed in 1739 and 1745, banning a wide range of amusements involving cards and dice. Humphrey Cleak invented E.O. to circumvent these bans, first introducing it at the tables in Tunbridge Wells. It was common knowledge that the odds favoured the bank, but the game nonetheless remained extremely popular. To maximize profits, Cleak formed a syndicate with the manager of the gaming room, Metcalfe Ashe. As Master of Ceremonies at Tunbridge Wells, Nash was called upon to settle a dispute over profits – and, with his keen eye for boosting his income, agreed to join the syndicate, receiving a cut of the profits. He failed to declare this interest, however, luring gamblers to the tables at the same time that – unbeknownst to them – he was profiting from their losses.

Nash's deal soured when he believed his partners in the syndicate had cheated him of his fair due, which he calculated at the enormous sum of 2,000 guineas. He brought a lawsuit against his partners in 1754, thereby publicly exposing how he had deliberately misled visitors for personal gain. Nash's reputation and his finances suffered following the revelation of his deception and corruption, and he was forced to sell many possessions and move to cheaper accommodation. However, despite this cautionary tale – and those of many others who went bankrupt – gaming continued to be a popular and acceptable spa entertainment.

A STAR IS BORN

Bath was a place where the fashionable could have their portraits painted. In November 1780 the *Bath Chronicler* carried an advertisement regarding an artist recently arrived in the city. It reported that his drawings could be seen at his home in St James's Parade, including two of 'two persons of the first distinction'.[33] This portraitist was a prodigiously talented 11-year-old boy, Thomas Lawrence, who had come to Bath with his father – a recent bankrupt – to seek his fortune executing portraits of the company.

Artists had long come to spa towns both to exhibit their works in galleries and to paint affluent patrons. Hundreds of artists worked in Bath during the eighteenth century, including William Hoare, who painted portraits of two of Bath's Masters of Ceremonies, Beau Nash and Samuel Derrick, while both Thomas Worlidge and Thomas Gainsborough settled in Bath in the 1750s. Gainsborough gained a following by painting various aristocrats – whom he charge 5 guineas for a portrait – as well as the beautiful soprano Eliza Linley (soon to elope with Sheridan). He left for London in 1774 but not before finishing his Bath career in a fashionable house in the Circus. Young Thomas Lawrence started his stellar career after leaving Devizes with his family. His father's coaching inn had gone bust, all his worldly possessions were auctioned in the summer of 1780, and Mr Lawrence recognized that the family fortunes lay with his beautiful and talented son. A tremendously precocious painter, the young Lawrence was soon completing three or four portraits a week. Lawrence would inevitably move to London to further his career, becoming the greatest portraitist of his generation.

Lawrence was not the only artist to make a name in Bath before taking London by storm. In September 1779 the curtain at the Theatre Royal in Bath rose on a new star – a 24-year-old actress named Sarah Siddons, who was playing Lady Macbeth. She had arrived in Bath a year earlier following a disastrous London debut as Portia at the Drury Lane Theatre in 1775. The reviews of that performance had been dire and wounding. 'There is not room to expect anything beyond mediocrity', ventured the reviewer for the *Middlesex Journal*, noting that her figure and face were commonplace, her voice monotone.[34] Siddons spent the next years in self-imposed exile, performing with small theatrical companies outside London. In 1778 she arrived at the Theatre Royal in Bath, where the local newspaper enthusiastically praised her as 'the most capital actress that has appeared here these many years'.[35] The pathos of her tragic performances moved audiences to tears, ultimately becoming so popular and successful that spa-goers began deserting the balls in the Assembly Rooms for the theatre. By the early 1780s she was the most successful and sought-after actress in English theatrical history – and in 1782 she would return to the Drury Lane Theatre, this time in triumph. Like those of Thomas Linley Jr and Thomas Lawrence, her talents were first appreciated in Bath.

Yet Bath gave the country more than just great musicians, painters and actors. The spa resort offered an ideal of civility and politeness, a place where the different classes and sexes could mix together, enjoying refined entertainments such as music and dance. After Bath, the vulgar and uncouth behaviour of earlier centuries was – at least in some respects – transformed into more sophisticated forms of social and cultural engagement as the waters not only cured scrofulous skin diseases but also improved British society itself. Nonetheless, even as spa towns such as Bath and Tunbridge Wells contributed to the nation's culture and civility, their many opportunities for social mixing and scandalous behaviour meant dubious conduct continued all too frequently, puncturing these dreams of refinement and self-improvement.

SIX

The Wells of Scandal

MEN (AND WOMEN) BEHAVING BADLY

Spas began as places of healing where the infirm and afflicted could seek a cure. But if the healing wells of the Middle Ages attracted the lame, the blind and the halt, the spas of the seventeenth and eighteenth centuries brought a different clientele, not only the wealthy and fashionable, as well as the newly minted 'middling sort', but also sometimes the unsavoury or opportunist. Spas became places where new maladies could take hold, moral as well as financial. As the eponymous heroine of Daniel Defoe's 1722 novel *The Fortunes and Misfortunes of the Famous Moll Flanders* puts it, a place like Bath was 'full of snares'.[1]

Beau Nash had tried to moderate social conduct so that relations between the classes and sexes were courteous and enjoyable. By and large he succeeded, such that, as Goldsmith claimed, 'the whole kingdom by degrees became more refined'.[2] Yet the spas offered far too many temptations, from gambling to sexual liaisons, for his ideal standards to be met by everyone. Bath and other watering holes certainly offered dangers as well as delights. Caddish fortune hunters and notorious cardsharps could trap or exploit the innocent or unwary, and the stories of lost fortunes and even lost lives – through duels and suicides – were regrettably common. Spas were

Thomas Rowlandson, *A Gaming Table at Devonshire House*, 1791.

dangerous places for the unwary and naive, but at the same time they offered freedoms not found elsewhere in British society, especially for women, with all of the attendant perils and exhilarations.

FORTUNE HUNTERS AND RAKISH WOMEN

Spa resorts inevitably attracted fortune hunters and various shady characters of both sexes. One such example was the handsome and extravagant Captain John 'Mad Jack' Byron. Born to an admiral in 1756, Mad Jack served in the Coldstream Guards and looked set for a distinguished military career like his father, before creating a scandal by conducting an affair with the wife of the Marquess of Carmarthen, whom he married following her divorce. After her death a few years later deprived him of her income – a handsome £4,000 per year – he turned up in Bath in search of another fortune. There he discovered Catherine Gordon, the 20-year-old daughter of the 12th Laird of Gight, whose body had recently been fished from the waters of the Avon. Raised since then by her strict Calvinist grandmother, Catherine was, according to a school friend, 'a romping, comely, good-humoured girl ... inclined to corpulency'.[3] She fell for Mad Jack's raffish charm and they were quickly married in Bath. A Scottish poet offered a bleak prediction: 'Ye've married, ye've married wi' Johnny Byron, / To squander the lands o' Gight awa.'[4] The prophecy was fulfilled soon enough as Mad Jack squandered her fortune and abandoned her, although not before fathering a club-footed child named George – the future poet Lord Byron.

Women were not the only ones who needed to guard against fortune hunters stalking the balls and gambling tables. 'So many rakish Women come down to Tunbridge, to make their Fortunes among us Men of Estates,' declares a character in Thomas Baker's 1703 play *Tunbridge Walks*, 'that if a Body ha'n't great care one may be stole.'[5] Moll Flanders may have noted that Bath was full of snares, but she was quite willing to go there to snare someone herself. She makes the trip to Bath because, as she puts it, 'though I was a woman without a fortune, I expected something or other might happen in my way that might mend my circumstances ... I went thither, indeed, in the view of taking anything that might offer.' She claims that she intended to pursue her interests 'in an honest way' but admits that soon she allowed herself to be guided in a different direction, ultimately becoming the mistress of a wealthy married gentleman who 'always supplied me with money to subsist me very handsomely'.[6]

An anonymous poem, 'The BATH Fortune-Hunter: Or, The Biter Bit', printed in 1735 and apparently based on the character of Defoe's Moll, illustrates the perils of the kinds of deception practised by fortune-hunters in Bath. It begins with a prostitute named Moll plying her trade in Drury Lane and subsequently departing for Bath to find a greater fortune. At the same time, a smartly dressed Irish gentleman with an air of superiority arrives in Bath, 'in Hopes to allure some *English* Dame'. The two fortune-seekers come together, each convinced of the other's wealth. Moll readily accepts his marriage proposal, but her beau abandons her after finding out that she is 'no more / Than a plain, downright, common Whore'.[7]

FLEECING SHARPERS

Gambling and spas were linked inextricably together. It was no coincidence that Beau Nash, who developed Bath, had started his career as a professional gambler. Indeed, one scurrilous tract called him (no doubt unfairly) 'a common Sharper' whose antics had reduced men to beggary and forced women into prostitution.[8] Nor is it a coincidence that Bath and other watering holes thrived at a time – prior to the anti-gambling Acts of 1739 and 1745 – when England experienced a mania for gambling of every sort. Gambling became popular following the Restoration, with White's Chocolate House in London a particularly notorious centre of operations. Women gambled as eagerly as men, and the classes mixed together at card tables. The *London Magazine*, reporting on Bath in 1737, claimed: 'Persons of all Characters and Denominations sit down to Cards from Morning to Night and Night to Morning.'[9] Elizabeth Montagu claimed that each morning the guests asked each other: 'How d'ye do?'[10] The temptation to gamble could be found everywhere in spa towns – so much so that Tunbridge Wells featured a row of shops selling jewellery and hosiery in which, besides buying brooches and stockings, one could play cards or dice.[11]

Gambling offered dangers as well as diversion. Unscrupulous gamesters were only too happy to relieve less experienced spa-goers of their money. In 1732 a poet described the 'strange promiscuous crew' one found at Scarborough, where 'Rakes and Bullies mingle with the Fair, / The fleecing Sharper and the unfledg'd Heir.'[12] One guide to Bath warned that those who loved to play and expected to win should understand 'in a *superlative degree*' that in Bath 'there are always *ingenious Men*, who live by their great *Talents for Play*', and who would 'make it a Rule to divide the many Thousands lost every year at Bath *among themselves only*.'[13] Sensible advice but, even so, many people ruined themselves. A particularly tragic case was that of Fanny Braddock, whose suicide – she hanged herself with a girdle from her closet door – was widely lamented in 1731. A resident of Bath, she had inherited £6,000 from her father, a general, 'but being a great Admirer of that hazardous Dependance *Gaming*, lately met with some unlucky Chance'. Through her gambling she lost, *The Gentleman's Magazine* reported, both her fortune and her reason.[14]

Then, too, there were the quarrels, one of which involved the victims at a card game in Bath throwing a cheating baronet from a first-floor window ('Never play so high again as long as you live!' one of his opponents later quipped following the defenestration).[15]

In the middle of another card game in Bath, a professional gamester, Baron Newman, had his hand pinned to the table by a fork. 'Monsieur Baron,' his assailant remarked, 'if you have not a card under your hand, I beg your pardon.' The fork was extracted, the hidden card revealed, and the baron thereafter forced to wear a muff to conceal his wound. He was a raffish type who, as *The Gentleman's Magazine* reported in his 1789 obituary, 'put a period to his existence' while in a drunken frenzy. The obituarist summed up his life with an arch set of italics: 'This man had been in his time very successful in the pursuit of his *honourable* occupation – that of a gamester – but had, like most of his fraternity, experienced the vicissitudes of fortune.'[16]

SWORDS AT DAWN

Other differences of opinion at the gaming table ended in duels. Captain Webster's was only the beginning of numerous duels and deaths. In November 1731 Lord Orrery wrote from Bath to an acquaintance reporting that a duel fought between two gamesters, a Mr Jones and a Mr. Price – the latter a gentleman's son – 'has put us in great confusion. Price is killed, & Jones has made his escape.'[17] Nash tried to halt these deadly altercations not only by banning swords but by having both parties arrested as soon as he heard of a challenge. It was one more way in which he hoped to bring his society out of the violence and vulgarity that had marked so much English public life. However, Nash himself was forced to fight a duel at Bath. After overhearing a young gallant making a rather lewd remark to a female bather, he threw the offender into the waters. Challenged to a duel, he suffered a wound in the arm but, apparently, enjoyed an enhanced authority as a man of spirit.[18]

Women surpassed even gambling as far as the causes of duels were concerned. One of the most famous duels in Bath occurred in 1772, almost twenty years after Nash's death. In 1770 the young

Richard Brinsley Sheridan, newly arrived in the city, fell in love with the beautiful 16-year-old singer Eliza Linley, daughter of the director of the Bath Concerts. There was much competition for Eliza's hand, including from a married man, a socially prominent friend of the Linley family from Glamorganshire named Captain Thomas Mathews. Eliza's father spurned all of her admirers except for one, a local landowner named Walter Long. The age difference – Long was forty-four years her senior – apparently made less of an impression on Mr Linley than Long's distinguished family history and £200,000 fortune.

The poet Richard Graves later mocked the affair in his 1783 poem, 'On an Old Gentleman Marrying a Fine Singing Girl', which features an old squire so enamoured of the song of a linnet that he captures the bird in a silken net and leaves it to flutter in a gilded cage. 'Ye swains the public loss deplore', the poet noted.[19] The actor and playwright Samuel Foote wrote *The Maid of Bath*, a comedy in which Kitty Linnet finds herself pressurized into marrying the elderly Solomon Flint. The play was performed at the Haymarket Theatre in London in June 1771, when the actors David Garrick and Richard Cumberland openly referred to the Linley affair. For her part, Eliza did not wish to marry such an older man and begged Long to retract his marriage proposal. Long did not welcome becoming a source of ridicule and agreed to rescind his offer, gallantly giving her £3,000 to repair any damage done to her reputation by the broken engagement.

Eliza's situation hardly improved, since Captain Mathews then began his pursuit in earnest, even threatening to kill himself if Eliza refused to return his passion. She therefore hatched a desperate plan by which, to escape from Mathews, she would flee the country and

Thomas Gainsborough, *Mrs Richard Brinsley Sheridan*, 1785–87. Gainsborough painted this portrait of the celebrated singer (née Eliza Linley) a dozen years after her marriage.

enter a convent in France. Sheridan offered to escort her, and so in March 1772 the pair of them slipped away from her home in the Royal Crescent under the cover of darkness and journeyed across the Channel to France. During the course of the flight Sheridan revealed his true feelings for her; the pair were secretly married by a priest in a village near Calais, and Eliza, according to plan, entered a convent in Lille. The escapade ended when her father pursued her to France and, anxious that she should fulfil her singing engagements, brought her home.

The aggrieved Captain Mathews took his revenge by (as Sheridan's biographer put it) throwing out 'reflections injurious to the reputation of Miss Linley and her lover' – reflections that soon found their way into a Bath newspaper.[20] Captain Mathews then left for London, followed by an indignant Sheridan, who, confronting him at his lodgings, threw down the gauntlet. After a farcical episode in which the two would-be duellists roamed Hyde Park in a fruitless search for a good place to do battle, the clash of swords eventually took place in the Castle Tavern in Henrietta Street in Covent Garden. Combat ended with the captain on the tavern floor, disarmed, pleading for his life and quickly agreeing to sign a retraction to be printed in the newspaper.

There the matter may have rested but for the mockery and chilliness to which Mathews found himself exposed when he returned to Glamorganshire. He therefore made his way back to Bath and challenged Sheridan, who, despite the protests of his friends, agreed to the highly unusual ritual of a second duel. On 2 July the parties met at four o'clock in the morning on Kingsdown, a hill outside Bath. A violent and bloody altercation followed, with both men breaking their swords from the force of combat. After much thrashing and rolling about on the ground, the pair were separated by their seconds. Faint from loss of blood, Sheridan was carried back to be patched up by a surgeon in Bath while his antagonist – perhaps feeling he had somewhat redeemed himself – heading for London. Over the following week the Bath papers eagerly printed updates on Sheridan's condition, which the patient enjoyed reading. 'Let me see what they report of me today,' he would remark each morning. 'I wish to know whether I am dead or alive.'[21]

A second wedding took place following the second duel as Eliza and Sheridan married in April 1773. The young couple bought a house in London, paying for it with the money given to her by Long. The marriage did not prove a happy one. Eliza never sang again – a linnet in a gilded cage. She suffered through Sheridan's affairs (and conducted one herself with Lord Edward Fitzgerald) before dying of tuberculosis in 1792, aged just 37. Sheridan meanwhile became the most celebrated playwright of his generation, having been amply supplied by his experiences in Bath with details for future plots.

'OF EITHER SEX WHOLE DROVES TOGETHER'

The very act of bathing – of removing one's clothes and submerging in warm water in the company of strangers, some of the opposite sex – was potentially fraught with both excitement and peril. Public bathing had long enjoyed an unsavoury reputation, suspected by St Augustine and Pope Gregory the Great as promoting sensuous pleasure over bodily health. Indeed, public baths (where people went to keep clean rather than heal themselves) had long been known as places of sexual liaison. In London, the bathhouses, or 'stews', of Southwark had been especially notorious. By Shakespeare's time, although the bathhouses had been shut for decades, the word 'stew' was synonymous with a brothel. When in *2 Henry IV* Falstaff talks about finding himself 'a wife in the stews' (1.2.52),[22] he is thinking of a woman of easy virtue. Prostitutes in Southwark became known as 'Winchester Geese' because during the fifteenth century the Bishop of Winchester regulated and profited from the stewholders.

In Bath, the mingling of men and women in the waters, together with the fact that they were exposed to the prying eyes of those in the surrounding buildings, was a cause of both titillation and concern. In *A Step to Bath*, the satirist Ned Ward claimed that some visitors to Bath relished the voyeurist pleasure of watching the bathers. 'The spectators in the galleries', he wrote, 'please their roving fancies with this lady's face, another's eyes, a third's heavy breasts and profound air.'[23] In the 1720s Daniel Defoe found that although 'the ladies and the gentlemen pretend to keep some distance, and each to their proper side', they mingled nonetheless, 'and talk, rally, make vows, and sometimes love'.[24] More indecorous breaches of etiquette

occurred if we are to believe the evidence of Thomas D'Urfey's 1701 comedy *The Bath: or, The Western Lass*, which features a naked and enthusiastic bather who, 'if there be e're a plump Londoner there ... he's on the back of her in a trice, and tabering her Buttocks round the Bath as if he were beating a Drum'.[25] Nude bathing still evidently took place on occasion, because in 1737 a law was passed stipulating that 'no Male Person above the age of Ten years shall at any time hereafter go into any Bath or Baths within this City by day or by night without a Pair of Drawers and a Waistcoat on their bodies.' Likewise,

'Public Bathing at Bath, or stewing alive', an 1825 engraving by Robert Cruikshank.

'no Female Person shall ... go into any Bath ... without a decent Shift on their bodies.'[26]

Various proposals were offered over the years to deal with problems caused by voyeurs and the mingling of the sexes. Archibald Cleland, appointed surgeon at Bath General Hospital in 1742, soon after it opened, proposed that the walls of the King's Baths should be raised high enough 'as to screen the people in the bath, from those without it'.[27] He may also have had in mind the protection of the bathers from another sort of attention, since they were prey not only to voyeurs but also to pranksters who pelted them with dead dogs and cats.[28]

A decade later Tobias Smollett, who had trained as a surgeon, made a similar series of recommendations for improving the conditions at Bath. A certain amount of segregation was observed. For example, the King's Bath featured an area in the middle, labelled 'the kitchen', where seats were reserved for women, while in the Queen's Bath a designated area, 'the parlour', was likewise women-only. However, Smollett suggested a more rigorous segregation by which the men and women bathed on alternate days. He also recommended that male guides should assist the men, and female guides the women.[29]

Yet the dangers lurking behind roving eyes and heaving bosoms could be found outside the baths as well. Indeed, temptation was everywhere. According to a character in Baker's *Tunbridge Walks*, a spa was 'a place wholly dedicated to Freedom'.[30] For another character, this freedom simply led to licentiousness, 'for what Lewdness is there this damn'd place don't countenance?'[31] The fact that people mixed together beyond the bounds of societal norms made spas susceptible to sexual intrigues. An 1691 poem on the wells in Islington described this mixing of men and women:

Of either sex whole droves together,
To see and to be seen flocked thither,

To drink – and not to drink the water,
And here promiscuously to chatter.

This promiscuous chattering between men and women could lead,
the poet believes, to dire circumstances. He gives the case of a
newly married couple who arrive at the wells:

For he perhaps in gazing round,
Has some new charming mistress found,
Whom he does 'fore his wife prefer,
So leaving spouse makes love to her.[32]

Charming mistresses were not difficult to find. The Abbé Prévost
claimed that in English spas there were 'Beauties of all ages who
come to show off their charms, young Girls and Widows in quest of
Husbands, and married Women who seek Solace for the unpleasant
ones they possess.'[33] Another writer claimed of Tunbridge Wells that
bachelors arrived with their mistresses, 'but marry'd People come
down single, Men without their Wives, and Women without their
Husbands; so that I suppose, whilst one part are there pleasing their
Palates with a new Dish, the other may be gone to the Bath to feast
their appetites with a fresh Dainty.'[34]

The waters of Scarborough, if we believe a poet, likewise
possessed restorative powers. In 1725 the anonymous rhymster
declared:

Thy Waters, Scarbro', quickly chace,
The Paleness from the Virgin's Face,
New paint her Cheek, new paint her Eye,
And raise again the Lover's Sigh.

He goes on to claim that these rejuvenating powers bring the
wealthy and the great to Scarborough to bathe in waters whose
'briny Foam increases their Desire' until they retire to 'quench each
other's Fire' in meadows or rocky caverns – a kind of Dionysiac
free-for-all on the Yorkshire coast.[35]

The reputations of spas for lechery and licence came not merely from the mingling of the sexes but also, in part, from their supposed abilities to make women fruitful.

Royal warrants could be found for such claims. In the summer of 1628 Henrietta Maria, 18-year-old wife of King Charles I, arrived in Wellingborough in Northamptonshire. She had been married to the king for three years without producing an heir, and so her arrival in Wellingborough – known for chalybeate spring waters that helped women to conceive – was no ordinary holiday. Lack of suitable accommodation meant she and her entourage camped in calico tents decorated with stars and gold lilies as she drank water from the Red Well. A few months later, she became pregnant; however, sadly, she lost the child, a boy, following a difficult labour. In the summer of 1629 she departed to recuperate in Tunbridge Wells, where once again, for lack of accommodation, she lived for six weeks in a tent on Bishop's Down Common. The following May she gave birth to another boy, the future King Charles II.

Three years after Henrietta Maria's visit, the mineral waters of Tunbridge Wells were celebrated in a treatise for their powers to help women conceive. A doctor from Ashford in Kent calling himself Lewis Rouse (also known as Lodwick Rowzee) advised the consumption of as many as fifteen pints a day to treat numerous ailments. 'In behalf of women,' he advised, 'there is nothing better against barrennesse, and to make them fruitfull.'[36] Over the next few decades, several more Stuart women would come to Tunbridge Wells with the particular plan of becoming fruitful and multiplying. In 1663 Charles II's wife, Catherine of Braganza, visited Tunbridge Wells. She had hopes of becoming pregnant and thereby, through an heir, increasing her influence and importance at the court. She conceived on three occasions but each time suffered a miscarriage.

In 1688 Charles II's niece, Princess Anne of Denmark, the future Queen Anne, visited Tunbridge Wells. Only 23, she had already suffered two miscarriages and two stillborn children, while two of her daughters had recently died in infancy. During her lifetime she was destined to loose eighteen children. The year after the 1688 visit she gave birth to a son, Prince William, Duke of Gloucester. William was a frail child. When, aged 9, he tripped and fell during an outing on the Upper Walk in Tunbridge Wells, Anne contributed money towards paving – what would become the Pantiles. William died in 1700, aged only 11. Anne never returned to the spa despite the fact that, in an attempt to entice her back, a cluster of birch trees, named the Queen's Grove, were planted on a nearby Common.

Besides Tunbridge Wells, Catherine of Braganza also visited Bath, likewise becoming famous for helping women conceive. Here, bathing rather than drinking supposedly aided conception. At the end of the century Robert Pierce would write that 'marry'd women' were often 'render'd fruitful by the Bath', and that many women who came for other complaints 'unexpectedly prov'd fruitful afterwards'.[37] Drinking spa waters was believed to open the kind of obstructions that

Queen Henrietta Maria, the young wife of King Charles I. Miniature by David des Granges, c.1636.

prevented conception. As Dr Robert Wittie wrote about the water of Scarborough in 1667: 'It is of thin parts, piercing into the most narrow and secret passages of the body, and is excellent in opening obstructions.'[38]

However, perhaps more germanely, thermal baths were also believed to possess an aphrodisiacal effect, stimulating the reproductive organs and providing them with heat.[39] A poem on the 'multiplying virtues' of Bath's waters suggested that cases of green sickness could be cured:

> Now she, who had been heretofore
> So meagre, pale, and wan,
> Digests her Food, and calls for more,
> Her Thoughts run all on MAN.[40]

The increase in sexual appetite supposedly brought on by a trip to a thermal bath, causing young maids to think of men, lent spas much infamy. Henrietta Maria was dissuaded from visiting Bath because of its squalor and reputation for lewdness in which 'both Sexes bathing by Day and Night naked'.[41] Indeed, certain English spas became so notorious for their aphrodisiacal powers, and for the ensuing lascivious behaviour, that even a Frenchman was shocked. In 1663 the comte de Cominges, French ambassador to the court of Charles II, claimed Tunbridge Wells should be renamed because of the way it ruined the reputation of women and girls. 'They should be called the Wells of Scandal,' he wrote, 'for they have gone right to ruining all women and girls of reputation (I mean such as had not their husbands with them).'[42] A few decades later, in 1687, a physician named Patrick Madan published *A Philosophical and Medicinal Essay of the Waters of Tunbridge*, in which he noted the power of the waters, when drunk, to make women 'fruitful and prolifick'. He offered various explanations for this phenomenon, noting that the waters enlivened 'the whole mass of blood' and the 'nobler parts' of the body and spirit. But sipping the waters also

A lecherous 'Doctor Doubledose' takes the pulse of an old woman while fondling a young lady behind her back, in this caricature by Thomas Rowlandson. Coloured etching, 1810.

'naturally incites and inspires men and women to amorous emotions and titillations' – sensations obviously conducive to procreation. Dr Madan therefore dubbed the mineral springs 'Cupid's well'.[43]

The link between fertility and spas was emphasized in a 1725 poem describing how barren wives arriving at a spa from London during 'Passion Week' soon enjoyed erotic experiences followed by the inevitable result when they were tended to by devoted doctors and the stimulating salts 'put their Blood in Motion'.[44] Doctors at spas certainly developed a certain reputation for ministering to female patients. A decade earlier a satirist noted that women visiting Tunbridge Wells frequently became pregnant 'provided they are but properly administered by a young vigorous Physician'. He noted that 'old grisly Galenists' did little business.[45]

These overly attentive young doctors, along with other obliging gallants, provided a rich comedic vein for authors to exploit, particularly during the Restoration. Parliament had banned plays in London during the Commonwealth of the 1650s. Although the ban was never wholly effective, with the Restoration of Charles II in 1660 drama returned with a vengeance. The lecherous king and his court – which featured notorious rakes such as John Wilmot, Earl of Rochester – enjoyed raunchy comedies (often performed on aptly named 'thrust stages' that protruded into the audience). A good many of these dramas were set in spas in order to bring together a broad spectrum of social types pursuing various amorous intrigues.

Many of these plays suggested that women who visited spas departed pregnant – either by accident or by design – with another man's child. The comedic possibilities were bawdily explored in Thomas Shadwell's 1672 play *Epsom-Wells*, in which a motley cast of characters pursue amorous adventures at the famous spa south of London. One character, Mr Kick, notes that 'many a London strumpet' comes to Epsom, to which his companion Ned Cuff replies: 'Others come hither to procure Conception.' 'Ay Pox,' declares Kick, 'that's not from the Waters, but something else that shall be nameless.'[46] King Charles II was present at the Duke's Theatre in London when the play was first performed in December 1672. He enjoyed it so much that that he attended two more performances, then arranged a showing for his wife, Catherine of Braganza. Having visited both Bath and Tunbridge Wells, Catherine no doubt knew very well the sort of scene described by Shadwell. But, given her miscarriages and fertility problems, the gesture might strike us as somewhat tactless – all the more so given that Epsom was a favourite resort of Charles's mistress, the actress Nell Gwynn.

The swaggering Kick and Cuff reappear in a poem by the Earl of Rochester. In Rochester's satire, a husband hoping for a male heir sends his wife to the spa. The narrator scoffs at his naive faith in the waters and ignorance of the true reason for his wife's sudden fertility:

Thy silly head! For here walk Cuff and Kick,
With brawny back and legs and potent prick,
Who more substantially will cure thy wife,
And on her half-dead womb bestow new life.
From these the waters get the reputation
Of good assistants unto generation.[47]

Before the end of the seventeenth century, Tunbridge Wells and Epsom had evidently developed a notorious reputation. A ballad about Tunbridge Wells published in 1678 alluded to the fact that it could cure both barrenness and the tedium of having a dull husband:

Then you that hither childless come
Leave your dull marriage behind you.
You'll never wish yourselves at home:
Our youth will be so kind to you.

An anonymous poem in *The Scarborough Miscellany*, published in 1732, makes a similar suggestion about the merits of Scarborough. The poem calls the 'blissful town' the 'rival of Bath', boasting that its 'more prolific Springs, / In hope of Heirs, the sterile Couple brings'. Few couples, it suggests, will leave discontented: 'For when the Waters fail, there's some will say, / The Cause has been remov'd ... some other Way.'[48] Or as a character states in Thomas Rawlins's 1678 comedy *Tunbridge Wells, or, A Day's Courtship*: 'Waters are but waters ... there goes more to the composition of an Heir, than minerals.'[49]

By the early decades of the eighteenth century, the plot in which a woman at a spa became pregnant in 'some other Way' was a reliable one. It features prominently in Eliza Haywood's 1725 pamphlet *Bath Intrigues*, which takes the form of a series of letters from the protagonist, J.B., who is visiting Bath, to a friend in London, Will. For the voyeuristic delectation of his friend, J.B. relates gossip and scandalous sexual misbehaviour, especially among the women. One story he tells is that of an attractive young woman, Camia, with a jealous and tight-fisted older husband. Camia is allowed to visit the Bath because her physicians assure her husband this is the only way she can produce an heir for him. The gentlemen of Bath therefore became 'not a little merry', resolved that they should leave no means untried to give him his heir, 'by a Remedy, which, 'tis probably, may be more effectual than the Waters'.[50]

WANTON DALLIANCES

The handsome doctors, as well as brawny libertines such as Kick and Cuff, no doubt delighted and appealed to some female spa-goers as much as the prospect of a child. The promise of amorous adventures, and of sexual contact *without* procreation, also brought many people to spas. A description by the satirist Ned Ward of the 'wanton dalliance' at the Cross Bath describes the erotically charged atmosphere of men and women mixing together — precisely the sort of saucy details coveted by Will in *Bath Intrigues*. Here the spa-goer encounters 'celebrated beauties, panting breasts and curious shapes, almost exposed to public view; languishing eyes, darting killing glances, tempting amorous postures' – all accompanied by music. He claimed that one could see in the corner of the bath 'an old lecher whose years bespoke him not less than three-score and ten, making love to a young lady not exceeding fourteen'.[51]

In Defoe's 1722 novel, Moll Flanders notes that at Bath 'men find a mistress sometimes, but very rarely look for a wife'.[52] As a character explains at the beginning of Thomas Baker's *Tunbridge Walks*, men visit spas such as Tunbridge Wells with the express purpose of courting women. A wide variety of women are on show, he claims, from 'wild Country-Ladies, with ruddy Cheeks like a *Sevil*-Orange', to 'Fat City-Ladies' and 'slender Court Ladies with *French* Scarfs, *French* aprons, *French* Night-Clothes and *French* Complexions'.[53]

Spas became popular as places of sexual intrigue and romantic entanglement because the ordinary rules of society were suspended as men and women – not to mention people of different social classes – mixed together. As the historian Phyllis Hembry has noted, 'large gatherings of mixed ranks at watering places presented a novel social phenomenon with no precedent for forms and routines of behaviour'.[54] Defoe noted that the social distinctions that held in London were relaxed in a place like Tunbridge Wells. 'Here you may have all the liberty of conversation in the world, and any thing that looks like a gentleman, has an address agreeable, and behaves with decency and good manners, may single out whom he pleases, that does not appear engag'd, and may talk, rally, be merry, and say any decent thing to them.'[55]

This liberty is enthusiastically described in Richard Ames's 1691 poem 'Islington Wells, or the Threepenny-Academy',[56] published only a few years after these springs in north London were rediscovered in 1683. Ames provides a vivid account of the heedless mixing of a broad spectrum of social types: doctors, apothecaries, ecclesiastics,

Mr Nunns with all respect begs leave to inform the
Public that he has engag'd

Miss KEMBLE,

Youngest Sister of

Mrs. SIDDONS;

She will make her first appearance in the Comedy
of the RIVALS.

THEATRE BRIDGNORTH

On WEDNESDAY Decr: 2d: 1795 will be perform'd a favorite COMEDY call'd

The RIVALS
Or a Trip to Bath.

The Part of Faulkland by Mr. Siddons.

Sir Anthony Absolute	Mr NUNNS
Capt: Absolute	Mr FAIRBAIRN
Davy	Mr FORESTER
Acres	Mr ROWLAND
Sir Lucius O' Trigger	Mr WHITMORE
Coachman	Mr HOLMES
Fag	Mr CLEATHER
Lydia Languish	Miss KEMBLE
(Being her first appearance on any Stage)	
Julia	Mrs NUNNS
Lucy	Mrs DUNN
Mrs Malaprop	Mrs MITTEER

After which a Musical Farce (and for the last time) call'd

The PURSE

The Part of Will Steady by Mr Siddons

	The Baron	Mr FORESTER	
Theodore	Mr FAIRBAIRN——Edmund	Mr	CLEATHER
Page	Miss PARSONS——Servant	Mr KELD	
	Sally	Mrs ROWLAND	

* * A Favorite PANTOMIME call'd

Harlequins Frolic

Or TRICK upon TRICK

(with entire new scenery and decorations Painted and design'd by
Mr Whitmore) is in Preparation and will be brought forward as
soon as Possible.

THE COMPANY WILL PERFORM ON

Mondays, Wednesdays, Fridays, and Saturdays.

tradesmen, tailors and country squires, but also predators such as sharpers, decoys and bullies – as well as, of course, 'Ladies, some Chast and others Common, / Young, Old, and many other Women'. All of them make their way to Islington Wells

> ... to make their Observation,
> Upon the Dresses of the Nation,
> Of either Sex whole Droves together,
> To see and to be seen flock thither,
> To Drink, and not to Drink the Water,
> And here promiscuously they Chatter.[57]

The narrator of 'Islington Wells' conceals himself in an arbour, the better to watch the company. Spas made possible all kinds of intrigue, spying and role-playing. Simply getting to a spa involved a woman in deception. The French art critic and historian Jean-Bernard, Abbé Le Blanc, wrote to a friend: 'The fair patient has had to feign illness, to win over the servants, to corrupt the doctor, to persuade an aunt, to deceive a husband, in a word to resort to all sorts of artifices to succeed.'[58] Once at a spa, the games and deceptions began in earnest. As one moralist complained, spas were full of 'Deluding Tricks and Shows', and of 'Dressings, Paints and Spells'.[59] New identities could be adopted and experimented with, as revealed in Sheridan's *The Rivals*, where Captain Jack Absolute, son of a wealthy baronet, masquerades as a more humble officer, Ensign Beverley, the better to fit the romantic notions of Lydia Languish.

A character in Baker's *Tunbridge-Walks*, Francis Maiden, also takes advantage of the liberties of the spa town to fashion a role for himself. Baker's dramatis personae identifies him as 'a Nice-Fellow, that values himself upon his Effeminacies'. He plays with pocket mirrors, curtsies, offers women advice about their dresses, paints

Playbill for a 1795 production of Sheridan's *The Rivals* (set in Bath).

his face, and earns the nickname Mrs Betty. 'Then I love mightily to go abroad in Women's Clothes', he declares, proudly noting that he once dressed in cherry-coloured damask, sat in the front box in the theatre, and was mistaken for 'a Dutch Woman of Quality'.[60] He is presented as a figure of fun ('prithee let's teaze him a little', one character says as Maiden appears), but the social composition of Tunbridge Wells is diverse enough for him to find like-minded companions – friends such as Beau Eithersex and Colonel Coachpole, with whom he enjoys cross-dressing parties in his chambers. The men play with fans, hold up their skirts, shriek like women and address each other as 'Madam'.

BLUESTOCKINGS AND SPAS

Freedom did not necessarily mean lewdness, licentious behaviour or clandestine affairs. Spas enabled women, in particular, to escape the everyday restrictions of their lives and interact with new and different sorts of people. They were not excluded from male company, as was so often the case at home, and they enjoyed participating in outings, social gatherings such as balls and concerts, and even simply in conversation. Spas also offered the opportunity for women to meet and befriend other women. They were likewise free to improve their minds by subscribing to circulating libraries in spa towns or attending lectures. 'I go every day to Mr. King's lectures', Elizabeth Montagu noted of her visit to Tunbridge Wells in 1742.[61]

The hostess and bluestocking Montagu was an inveterate spa-goer. She took the affable social mixing she enjoyed there into a wider society and, in doing so, helped to create a new space for women. Montague had been born into an affluent and aristocratic family in 1718, and as a girl she received a good education in Latin, French and Italian (her stepgrandfather, Conyers Middleton, was a celebrated Cambridge scholar). She also received, thanks to her energetic personality, the nickname 'Fidget'. She became friends with Lady Margaret Harley, daughter of the Earl of Oxford, likewise a lively and well-educated young woman. After Lady Margaret married William Bentinck, Duke of Portland, in 1734, Elizabeth paid regular visits to them at their country seat, Bulstrode Park in Buckinghamshire, enjoying the mix of aristocratic company and intellectual conversation in which men and women participated as equals. In 1742 she married a much older man, John Montagu, MP for Huntingdon and owner of land and collieries in Northumberland and Yorkshire, as well as of a country pile in Berkshire, Sandleford Priory, near Newbury. After their only child died in infancy, Elizabeth spent much time away from her husband, regularly taking the waters in both Bath and Tunbridge Wells. In the summer of 1752, after appearing in Tunbridge Wells dressed in a Chinese robe brought back by her brother from the East, she wrote: 'I appeared in full Chinese pomp at the ball, my gown was much liked.'[62]

Montagu hosted friends in Tunbridge Wells during the summers, when she rented a house for the season and then enticed them to join her. She continued the practice at her London home, in Hill Street, Mayfair. She quickly became famous as a society hostess, combining the social mixing she enjoyed at the spas with the intellectual and literary conversations she remembered from Bulstrode Park. She banned card-playing and heavy drinking at her salons – two of the chief causes of problems in spas – and instead encouraged her guests to debate literary or philosophical topics (politics was usually avoided). These salons were attended by such luminaries as David Garrick, Samuel Johnson, Sir Joshua Reynolds (who painted her portrait) and Horace Walpole. Likewise present were many women, including the novelists Fanny Burney and Sarah Fielding, the poet and playwright Hannah More, the author and diarist Hester Thrale (who hosted soirées of her own), and Montagu's close friend, the vivacious Irish hostess Elizabeth Vesey. By the 1760s Montagu and her female companions became known informally as 'the bluestockings', a term perhaps invented by Vesey as a way of describing their informality of dress – blue worsted rather than fine silk.

In 1783 a visitor to one of these gatherings wrote that one met with 'a charming variety of society' in them – 'the Learned, the witty, the old & young, the grave, gay, wise & unwise, the fine bred Man & the pert coxcomb; The elegant female, the chaste Matron, the severe prude, & the pert Miss'.[63] In other words, the mixed company was much the same as what one found at a spa during the season, albeit with an intellectual gloss added thanks especially to Montagu, Thrale and Vesey.

Singer Elizabeth Sheridan (*centre*), society leader Elizabeth Montagu (*seated centre right*) and writer Hannah More (*standing, near right*) feature in this portrayal of leading 'bluestockings', each representing one of the nine muses. Painting by Richard Samuel, 1778.

SEVEN

'I do like to be beside the seaside'

A DOSE OF VITAMIN SEA

Between 1750 and the outbreak of war in Europe in 1793, spa resorts flourished as holiday destinations. Their success was helped by improvements to the roads of England and the provision of more horses to pull public and personal carriages. Indeed, the roads were so greatly improved that in 1794 one traveller claimed the highways were 'so multiplied and extended as to form almost an universal plan of communication through the kingdom'.[1] Spa-goers took full advantage of these easier conditions, and commercial coaches ferried visitors quickly and efficiently to the resorts. By the 1880s stage coaches from London to Cheltenham travelled at a respectable 5½ miles per hour.[2]

Transportation by the waterways likewise improved, enabling the supply of spa towns with building materials, coal, food and luxury goods. Meanwhile the Enclosure Acts, which facilitated the private ownership of formerly common land, made possible the creation of private estates at Buxton, Cheltenham and Harrogate, where new spa resorts exploited mineral springs. Towns expanded around spas, increasing employment in the service industry, and the demand for

Benjamin West's depiction of the beach at Ramsgate, 5 miles from Margate, featuring bathing machines and nude swimmers.

building new accommodation grew. In Bath alone, an estimated 5,000 houses were built between 1720 and 1800 to accommodate both the burgeoning population and the hoards of visitors. The spa industry became so profitable for Bath's tradesmen, hostellers and medics that a second season was introduced. Coal from the nearby Mendip Hills provided heat for patrons in the colder months; it was transported to Bath, first by horse and cart, and then by barge following the opening of the Somerset Coal Canal in 1805. Retailers from Cheltenham and Bristol Hotwells moved to Bath for the winter season. In the north of England, due to inclement weather, the season was later than in the south. The exception was Matlock, whose season, due to the town's sheltered position, commenced in April. Buxton's season was in June, and Harrogate's in July.

The War of the First Coalition (1793–97) and the Napoleonic Wars (1799 and 1815) caused a recession in spa promotion. A guidebook from shortly after this time described how Matlock suffered a drop in visitors because of the 'desolating scourge of war'.[3] Building halted in Bath and Bristol, where attendances also waned. The popular Marshall Circulating Library in Bath went bankrupt due to a lack of subscribers. By the time the war finally ended in 1815, tastes began to change as – suddenly able to travel abroad thanks to the Treaty of Paris – people journeyed to the Continent, including to its spas. However, patrons also began travelling to newer, recently expanded and more spacious spas, such as those in Cheltenham and Leamington. They were also introduced, as the decades progressed, to a whole new series and variety of spa experiences. Between 1800 and 1850, seventy new spa centres opened throughout the British Isles. Many of these were spas with a difference. If the healthful aspect of visiting a spa consisted, in the eighteenth century, of drinking water in a pump room and perhaps taking a dip in the waters, spa-goers in the nineteenth century became more adventurous, experimenting with different types and temperatures of water. They also discovered different places, as those seeking health and recreation discovered Britain's coastline.

A DIP IN THE WAVES

Scarborough has some of the coldest waters in the United Kingdom. And yet it was also, perhaps unexpectedly, among the first places where English spa-goers took to the waves. The satirist was not exaggerating when, in 1725, he described visitors to Scarborough Spa disporting themselves in the 'briny Foam' — although whether such a shivering experience would (as he claimed) increase their desire and lead to trysts stolen in rocky caverns is anyone's guess.[4] Supping both chalybeate and saline spa water at Scarborough had been popular since the two springs were discovered at the bottom of Scarborough cliffs and endorsed by Dr Robert Wittie in 1660. Wittie also was the first doctor to recommend sea bathing for health and pleasure, claiming that it could cure the gout. Sarah Churchill, Duchess of Marlborough, declined to enter the waves during her visit in 1732, even though she was suffering from gout. However, that summer the more youthful Isabella Montagu, Duchess of Manchester, was taking a daily dip. So too did Matthew Bramble in *The Expedition of Humphrey Clinker*. However, Clinker, his devoted servant (and, spoiler alert, his illegitimate son), mistakenly believed his master was drowning and therefore, to Bramble's fury, pulled him stark naked from the waters. The composer George Frederick Handel visited in the summer of 1745, but the waters apparently did him little good since he returned to London and 'talk'd much of the precarious state of his health'.[5]

Taking the plunge in the cold waters off the Yorkshire coast was obviously a different proposition to paddling in the warm waters of Bath, which reached temperatures of 45°C (113°F), or even in one of the cold-water baths such as those at Matlock or Ilkley. However, the potential dangers of bathing were made clear in the summer of 1785 when a man drowned on a Sunday morning in the public baths in Coldbath Fields in Clerkenwell when the attendant went to answer a knock at the door.[6]

Sea bathing was especially dangerous because so few people knew how to swim. During the sixteenth century swimming had generally been scorned by the English as an ungentlemanly pursuit; other physical activities such as archery, tennis, swordplay and wrestling were preferred. In 1531 Sir Thomas Elyot noted that swimming was little known or practised, 'specially amonge noble men', and that 'perchance some reders wyll litle esteme it'.[7] Cambridge University banned swimming in 1571, and in *Positions*, a treatise on education published in 1581, Richard Mulcaster expressed ambivalent feelings. He allowed that swimming could save a person from danger, and that it was 'very good to remoue the headache, to open the stuffed nostrilles, and therby to helpe the smelling', but he feared that 'rotten and corrupt vapours' might enter the body through the pores. He also believed that the sinews could perish from the cold and moisture, and ultimately he maintained that 'all swimming must needes be ill for the head' because of the 'continuall exhalation which ascendeth still from the water'.[8]

Swimming did receive the endorsement of a Cambridge fellow named Everard Digby, an eccentric who evidently enjoyed aquatic activities since he fell foul of the University authorities for, among other things, taking his students fishing when they were supposed to be in the chapel. In 1587 he published *De Arte Natandi* (The Art of Swimming) in the hope of making swimming a fit skill for gentlemen. He included more than forty woodcuts and instructions to the book to teach people different strokes, the most basic of which were a breast stroke (albeit without kicking the legs) and the doggy paddle. He also suggested using inflated pigs' bladders as personal flotation devices. The work was translated into English in 1595; however, few people over the following century knew how

Illustration from the earliest swimming manual to be published in England, *De Arte Natandi libro duo* by Everard Digby, c.1587.

to swim with any proficiency. During the 1720s Benjamin Franklin, who learned to swim as a child in Boston, amazed English onlookers by swimming in the Thames from Chelsea to Black-friars, 'performing on the way many feats of activity, both upon and under water'.[9] His feats in the river as well as his success in teaching others meant he contemplated opening a swimming school in London.

However, it was not Franklin but rather spas such as those in Scarborough and Southampton that ultimately got the English into the waves. Bathers and swimmers were largely absent from the shorelines and beaches until the middle of the eighteenth century, when, thanks to these spas, seawater came to be associated with health rather than with noxious exhalations and weakened limbs. The physician John Speed described the physical benefits of bathing in cold seawater. Salt was a stimulus as well as 'an efficacious Cleaner of the Glands of the Skin', and those emerging from the waves perceived 'a Kind of Firmness' in their skin and a heat over the entire surface of their bodies – 'a Forerunner of re-established Health'. If for some time this heat did not arrive spontaneously, bathers were to take moderate exercise afterwards. 'Sea Water therefore is not simply a cold Bath,' he concluded, 'but a *cold medicated* Bath'. He admitted, however, that it was impossible for physicians to predict or determine how many immersions might be necessary to cure a particular disease in an individual patient – yet many patients 'are so silly as to expect this'.[10]

Bathing in the sea had become popular enough by 1750 that Dr Speed could write that 'the Use of Sea Water is grown into a Fashion', and that many patients flocked to the Hampshire coast.[11]

Southampton, a garrison town, had become a spa resort a decade earlier when a chalybeate spring was found, and then, after 1750, when Frederick, Prince of Wales, arrived in town to bathe in the sea. The tradition was continued, following Frederick's death in 1751, by his sons. Included among them was the future George III, who would later also bathe in the waters of Weymouth (his favourite seaside resort) during his periodic episodes of mental illness. The king much preferred seawater immersion to another treatment prescribed to him by his doctors, that of being tied to a chair in front of a fire, or, as he put it, 'roasted alive for

Detail of spa and bathing machines at Scarborough, from a 1745 engraving by Samuel and Nathaniel Buck.

six hours'.[12] On a number of occasions he even convened his court in Weymouth.

Those who flocked to Scarborough or Southampton did not need to know how to swim. In 1758 a Mr Dubourg invented a 'cork-waistcoat', a flotation device aimed at 'all those who resort to bathing places for the benefit of their health', including 'the most timorous and delicate', who would now be able to 'boldly venture with one of these waistcoats into a rough sea'.[13] A more successful invention from around the same time was the bathing machine. Indeed, bathing in seawater was made possible by the appearance at seaside resorts of bathing machines, described by one bather as 'a curious contrivance of Wooden Houses moveable on wheels'.[14] These contraptions had appeared in Southampton by the 1750s, thanks to John Martin, a local entrepreneur who also built a bathhouse and an assembly room. A small wooden cabin with a pitched roof and set of doors was mounted on a wheeled under-carriage, to which a horse was harnessed. It was pulled into the sea with the bather inside, and once it had been rolled into position the bather descended a set of wooden steps and, helped by an attendant, entered the waves. Bathers always exited on the seaward side, to

avoid the prying gazes of anyone on shore. Swimming costumes consisted of much the same type of garment as found in Bath.

Decorum could be further preserved by such devices as the 'modesty hoods' that a glove maker in Margate, a Quaker named Benjamin Beale, invented in the middle of the eighteenth century – an awning that could be lowered to provide privacy for the bather once immersed in the water. Blackpool featured bathing machines towed by horses, as well as sheds in which bathers could change, although, as a writer pointed out in 1789, 'a few travel from their apartments in their water dress'. The city fathers hit on an interesting expedient for sparing the blushes of female bathers. When a bell rang the women were free to take to the waters. Segregation was strictly enforced: 'If a gentleman is seen upon the parade he forfeits a bottle of wine.'[15]

Bathing machines were used on English beaches well into the nineteenth century (and a few even survived into the twentieth). By-laws in Brighton in the 1870s carefully governed their use, with male and female bathers assigned separate machines at stations along the seafront – 182 for women and 162 for men. The machines, privately owned and rented by the half-hour, were to display, 'on some conspicuous part', either 'For Ladies' or 'For Gentlemen'. Ladies were expected to wear 'gowns or dresses' in the water, the gentlemen such coverings 'as will prevent indecent exposure of the person'. However, the by-law states, intriguingly, that 'no person shall bathe from any machine after seven o'clock a.m. without wearing gowns, drawers, or some such suitable covering' – raising the possibility that skinny-dipping was permitted late at night and early in the morning.[16] Most swimming or bathing in rivers or at the seaside had been done in the nude, as the woodcuts in Digby's treatise indicate: they show gentlemen in lace ruffs peeling off their doublets and hose before disporting themselves in the waves completely starkers.

Robert Wittie had advised his patients against drinking seawater. However, Dr Speed, a few decades later, advised precisely that, noting that by coming into contact with the obstructed intestinal glands it operated as a purge 'both by Stool and Urine'. He offered a number of case studies in which drinking seawater, and often bathing it in too, helped his patients with various conditions. He was cautious, however, warning that those with 'hot Constitutions should never drink it, for it corrodes the Intestines as such, and by a constant Use punishes them severely'.[17]

Dr Speed's treatise on seawater was translated from its original Latin and published by Richard Russell, who likewise became famous for advocating drinking and bathing in seawater. Born in Lewes in 1687, Russell received an impeccable medical education, first in London and then at the University of Leiden, before returning to practise in Lewes in 1724. After observing how people on the coast drank seawater to treat their stomach and intestinal complaints, he began recommending it to patients sent by their doctors from London to enjoy the sea air in Brighthelmstone (now Brighton), a few miles from Lewes. He soon had many of these patients bathing in the sea too, since his treatment involved complete submersion in seawater as well as, in some instances, drinking up to a pint of it daily.

In 1750 Russell published a Latin treatise *De tabe glandulari, sive, De usu aquæ marinæ in morbis glandularum dissertatio*; after the proprietor of a mineral water warehouse in London published a pirated English edition in 1752, Russell quickly issued his own translation, *A Dissertation Concerning the Use of Sea Water in the Diseases of the Glands* (to which he appended Dr Speed's treatise). He believed the waters to be especially helpful to treat scurvy, jaundice, the King's Evil, leprosy and consumption, although his preface stated that 'so powerful a Medicine' was bound to have far more extensive use.

Indeed, he believed that the 'ominiscient Creator of all Things' seemed to have designed the oceans 'to be a Kind of common Defence against the Corruption and Putrefaction of Bodies'.[18]

The key ingredient in seawater was, of course, salt, which Russell noted prevented putrefaction. He was aware that drinking seawater could prove problematic since it has a higher salt content than we can safely consume (urine cannot be produced by the kidneys if there is a concentration of salts of more than 2 per cent, whereas seawater is made up of approximately 3 per cent). When Russell advised patients to drink a pint of seawater, he was sensible enough to recommend never to drink seawater solely. After patients were bled, they were offered other remedies, such as wine or water-based liquids, to counteract dehydration. Dr Speed noted approvingly the habit of the Ancient Romans and Greeks of mixing seawater with wine or honey, and then afterwards having the patient drink chicken or fish broth.

Dr Russell's treatise contains numerous case studies of patients successfully treated for various afflictions, including a 12-year-old girl cured of leprosy through a regime of a half-pint of seawater and various medicines such as calomel, camphire and viper's flesh. He even cautiously advised a treatment for gonorrhoea: a pint of seawater taken with various potions. Seawater could be introduced into the body through various means. A fisherman suffering from colic and severe constipation was given boiled chamomile flowers in a pint and a half of seawater, which was administered with a clyster – that is, as an enema. Four hours after the enema the patient was to drink a draught of oil of manna and sweet almonds, 'but as I heard afterwards,' he wrote, 'the Draught was omitted, because the Patient found the Clyster alone had a sufficient Operation'.[19]

The demand for his treatments soon inspired Dr Russell to purchase property along the base of a cliff on the eastern edge of Brighthelmstone – the start of what would become Brighton's long reign as a seaside resort. He also recommended the chalybeate

Mermaids at Brighton by William Heath, c.1829.

waters from a spring in Hove known as St Ann's, thought particularly useful for consumptive patients. He enclosed the well with a wooden structure and installed a basin specifically for his patients. He included in his treatise a list of no fewer than eighty-seven places in England where mineral waters could be drunk, with special reference to their salt content.

ON MARGATE SANDS

Another advocate of seawater was the Quaker physician and philanthropist John Coakley Lettsom. Born in 1744 in the Virgin Islands, where his father owned a plantation, Lettsom came to England as a child (and he would later, in a typically humane gesture, free all of the slaves on his father's estate). Following medical studies in Edinburgh and Leiden – where Russell had also matriculated several decades earlier – he set up a lucrative practice in London, treating many high-society patients and carrying on correspondence with, among others, Benjamin Franklin, Erasmus Darwin and George

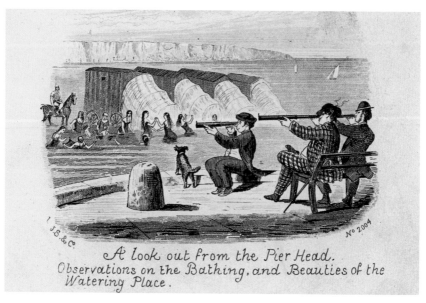

*A look out from the Pier Head.
Observations on the Bathing, and Beauties of the
Watering Place.*

Three men look through telescopes at young women bathing in the sea in this humorous print. Undated wood engraving.

Washington. In 1772 he published his medical dissertation from Leiden as *The Natural History of the Tea Tree with Observations on its Medical Qualities, and Effects of Tea-drinking* — which maintained the brew made its drinkers weak and effeminate. Dr Lettsom forever concerned himself with the public good, the poor as well as his affluent patients. 'Few, I believe, have more truly passed their lives in doing good to man', a friend wrote to him in 1810.[20] It was with this sort of philanthropy in mind that in 1791 he purchased 2 acres of land in Margate for the founding of the Royal Sea-bathing Infirmary, expressly for the benefit of the poor of London. Margate had a long tradition of seawater bathing, the first enclosed seawater bath (accommodating one person at a time) having opened in 1736, supplied by a conduit from the sea. The concern was operated by a local carpenter named Thomas Barber, who advertised the privacy and convenience of his establishment, which allowed bathers to take the waters no matter what the weather or state of the tide.

The Royal Sea-bathing Infirmary opened in the summer of 1796 with the stated aim of 'giving our poor Fellow-creatures an Opportunity thereby of removing their Maladies'.[21] A report issued a few months after the opening happily declared that most of the patients, who had 'laboured under long-continued Maladies', were restored to health thanks to 'one Course of Bathing; and, on intermediate days, drinking Sea-water'.[22] Sores were treated with compresses of marine plants, while the fresh air of the coast – the spot in Margate had been specially selected for its breezes – returned others to health.

Funded by subscriptions, the hospital originally hoped to accommodate ninety-two patients, but this proved too ambitious, and in the end only thirty patients could be in residence at a time. All of them were admitted on a recommendation from a doctor for a maximum period of six weeks. Before leaving Margate they were to give thanks in the parish church. The wards opened onto piazzas so that the beds could be pushed outside. Special nurses oversaw the sea bathing. Patients arrived at the shore in bathing machines pulled by horses. The perils of conducting patients into the waves was illustrated in a letter a friend wrote to Dr Lettsom from Aldeburgh in 1810: he described how he 'met with an accident in bathing, being driven by a wave against the ladder of the machine, which put out my right shoulder'.[23] He noted that at least he had not been swept out to sea. In 1853 horse-driven pumps forced seawater into an indoor saltwater pool so treatment could continue through the winter months. By 1900 the hospital had expanded with new wards, a house for the governor and a school.

The bracing air of Margate was so renowned for its recuperative qualities that in 1921 a distinguished visitor arrived in town. Having suffered a nervous breakdown in London, the poet T.S. Eliot came with his wife Vivien. In October they took a room at the Albemarle Hotel, and although Eliot neither bathed nor drank seawater he spent much time in the open air in a shelter on the seafront. It was here that he wrote part of his masterpiece, *The Waste Land*, including a reference to Margate Sands.[24]

ARTIFICIAL WATER

Brighton's seawater continued to be used for bathing and drinking for many years following Dr Russell's death in 1759. The Irish physician Anthony Relhan, who moved to Brighton in 1759, promoted the virtues of its waters as a treatment for invalids in *A Short History of Brighthelmstone*, published in 1761. In 1769 a doctor named John Awsiter constructed the resort's first baths in a building featuring six cold baths, a hot bath and separate areas for showering and sweating. All were supplied with water from the sea, with the heated waters aimed at helping patients sweat out their 'poisonous humours'.[25]

The German Spa, Queen's Park, Brighton, 1841, published by C. Andrews. Friedrich Struve created this successful spa in 1825.

A new attraction for spa-goers in Brighton, the Royal German Spa, was opened in 1825 by a German doctor and apothecary from Neustadt named Friedrich Struve. In 1808, while conducting a laboratory experiment, Struve had accidentally poisoned himself with hydrocyanic acid, causing paralysis in his lower limbs. After successful treatment drinking the waters at the famous spas in Marienbad and Carlsbad he came up with the idea of creating mineral waters by artificial means. The upshot of his experiments was an effervescent distilled water enriched with minerals and trace elements. He opened his first facility in Dresden in 1818, followed by ones in Leipzig and Berlin, before he arrived in Brighton, where he used not seawater but rather water from an artesian well that he sank deep into the chalky cliffs. After gaining the patronage of King William IV, his establishment at the southern end of Brighton Park (now Queen's Park) was christened the Royal German Spa.

Struve's spa became an attraction not merely for patients sent by their doctors but also for visiting Londoners eager to try something new and different. He constructed a classical-style building consisting of six Ionic fluted columns that fronted the main room where water, impregnated with gases from a gasometer, flowed from silver or glass spouts and was served to customers by well-dressed

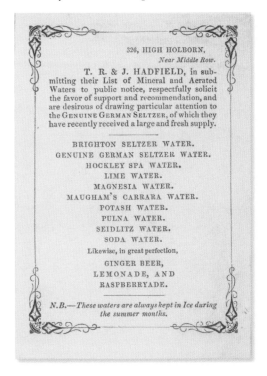

326, HIGH HOLBORN,
Near Middle Row.

T. R. & J. HADFIELD, in submitting their List of Mineral and Aerated
Waters to public notice, respectfully solicit
the favor of support and recommendation, and
are desirous of drawing particular attention to
the GENUINE GERMAN SELTZER, of which they
have recently received a large and fresh supply.

BRIGHTON SELTZER WATER.
GENUINE GERMAN SELTZER WATER.
HOCKLEY SPA WATER.
LIME WATER.
MAGNESIA WATER.
MAUGHAM'S CARRARA WATER.
POTASH WATER.
PULNA WATER.
SEIDLITZ WATER.
SODA WATER.
Likewise, in great perfection,
GINGER BEER,
LEMONADE, AND
RASPBERRYADE.

N.B.—*These waters are always kept in Ice during
the summer months.*

An undated trade card from the London firm of T.R. & J. Hadfield, listing their impressive range of spa waters.

female attendants. The pump room was open between 8 a.m. and 10 p.m. from May to September, with its waters advertised as 'offering every facility for taking a course of Mineral Waters in precisely the same perfection, and with the same benefit, as the natural Springs'.[26] At the height of its popularity, carriages filled with passengers waited their turn to drink the imitation Continental waters, queuing all the way to the seafront. Struve's waters were also bottled at the source and sold, both at the Royal German Spa and through a various dealers in London. Struve & Co. also sold bottled water from Continental spas such as Vichy, Spa, Marienbad and Seltzer. By the 1860s his waters were so popular that various imitations were sold under names such as 'Brighton Seltzer' and 'Brighton Vichy' – a practice Struve & Co. sought to counter by giving each of their bottles a distinctive red-ink stamp on the cork. After sales declined, the pump room closed its doors in 1886, but Hooper Struve & Co., as it became known, continued to produce bottled mineral water and other fizzy drinks in Brighton well into the twentieth century.

BRINE BATHS OF DROITWICH

In the autumn of 1831 a ship from the Baltic Sea docked in Sunderland, with the sailors suffering from a terrifying new disease: cholera. The disease quickly spread through Britain, leaving behind a death toll of at least 32,000 people. Various preventatives and cures were proposed, such as beef broth, brandy and laudanum. Although these treatments did little good, a more effective one was discovered in the Worcestershire town of Droitwich, situated in the valley of the Salwarpe river.

The seaside was not the only place to find salty water. The Ancient Romans had given Droitwich the name Salinae, the place of salt. Salt from its brine springs had been harvested since the Iron Age, and the Domesday Book named it as the most important

salt-producing town in England. During the cholera epidemic of
1831–32, so many people in the town fell victim to the disease
that a disused salt works was turned into a hospital. On admission,
patients were routinely bathed in hot water, but when the water
ran out due to the large numbers of the sick and dying, they were
bathed instead in brine from the springs – and began to make
remarkable recoveries.

The key to their recoveries was the salt in Droitwich's waters,
which would have helped with their rehydration. Today the World
Health Organization states that the treatment of cholera requires the
prompt administration of oral rehydration salts to replace lost fluids.

Later investigations would reveal that the water from the springs
at Droitwich contains four times the concentration of salt as the
Dead Sea and as much as twelve times that of seawater. An 1875
guidebook claimed that every gallon of brine – which engines
pumped from subterranean rivers a hundred feet beneath the surface
– contained 20,000 grains of salt.[27]

After the dramatic discovery of the advantages of bathing in
Droitwich's salty waters, a local physician named Sir Charles
Hastings, the first president of the British Medical Association,
became an ardent supporter of its medicinal properties. Hastings
campaigned for the construction of public baths, which in 1836
opened in St George's Square at the back of the George Inn (later
the Royal Hotel), complete with an assembly room. When the
railway reached Droitwich in 1849, a local businessman, one W.G.
Gabb, floated a joint-stock company so the baths could be further
expanded and improved. Gabb, a talented entrepreneur, even
persuaded the Great Western and Midland Railways to issue conces-
sions on rail tickets from Birmingham to the Brine Baths. By the
1870s the baths were being run by W.H. Bainbrigge, who further
developed the site, making the baths 'suitable for all classes'. His
establishment featured a Turkish bath, sitz bath, hot and cold brine

sprays, as well as a brine swimming bath 30 feet wide by 70 feet long. As an 1875 guidebook reported: 'They are substantial, commodious, and fitted with every necessary comfort.' It also noted that those who came to seek relief included 'noblemen, ladies of rank, and first-class visitors', that many of these invalids had already gone to other English and Continental spas, and that Droitwich water did them 'more good than all the others put together'.[28] The baths publicized testimonies of those who had been cured of afflictions such as rheumatism, rheumatic fever, sciatica and gout, as well as 'young persons with no appetite, bloodless almost, and looking pale and weak'.[29] The Royal Brine Spa proved healthy for local hostelries too, and for much of the year every bed in Droitwich was booked.

The 'Salt King', John Corbett, was likewise responsible for developing the spa at Droitwich. Born in 1817, Corbett had earned a fortune by using new engineering methods at the Stoke Prior salt works near Droitwich, which he purchased in 1852. He quickly became the world's largest producer of salt, manufacturing 200,000 tons per year. A great philanthropist and early advocate of women's suffrage, Corbett was a model employer, offering his workers such amenities as gardens, schools and a club house. He also contributed funds towards the University of Birmingham, the University College of Wales and the Bromsgrove Cottage Hospital. In 1889, when he was serving the area as Liberal MP, he gave the Old Saline Baths a makeover, fitting them out with hydrotherapy equipment and renaming them St Andrew's Brine Baths. For his wife, who had been raised in Paris, he constructed the Chateau Impney on the outskirts of the town, a magnificent French Renaissance-style home. It failed to assuage her homesickness: the couple would eventually separate. It became a hotel, and there is still an outlet for the brine waters in the hotel grounds.

A 1953 advertisement for Droitwich Spa.

DROITWICH SPA

the Brine Spa

SAL·SAPIT·OMNIA

EIGHT

The Water Cure

THE VICTORIAN MANIA FOR HYDROTHERAPY

A visitor to an English spa in the 1750s – to Tunbridge Wells or Bath – would have anticipated a fairly relaxed, and even lax, regime of drinking, and perhaps even bathing in, waters rich in iron or sulphur. Food, drink, comfort and entertainment were limited only by their budgets or by the amenities of the spa. A visitor to an English spa in the 1850s was in for quite a different experience. The patient could expect to be force-fed flasks of water, wrapped in wet blankets, pummelled by cataracts of water, plunged into cold baths, marched up hills, and fed an unrelentingly bland diet of bread, mutton and treacle. Such was the world of hydrotherapy – the water cure.

POURING COLD WATER ON IT

In 1814 Vincent Priessnitz, a farmer's son from Gräfenberg (now in the Czech Republic), watched a roebuck heal its wounded limb by repeatedly bathing in a local pond. Vincent realized that water had healing powers when he successfully treated his own sprained wrist by immersing it in water. The immersion caused what he called an *Ausschlag*, or eruption – the expelling of unhealthy matter – which

Burrow's Malvern Table Waters advertisement, early twentieth century.

was followed by a sudden improvement. He treated himself in similar fashion a short time later when, run over by a hay wagon, he healed his broken ribs by swaddling himself in damp bandages and drinking abundant quantities of water (although he could do nothing for his three missing teeth, knocked out in the mishap). His reputation for healing with water rapidly spread, and he began curing people and animals using his new-found skills, applying wet bandages to sprains, cuts and bruises. The appearance beneath the bandages of the eruptions – boils and abscesses – convinced him that the water possessed the power to draw some sort of injurious foreign matter from the body. At the age of 22 he opened a sanatorium in an extension to his father's house, and patients flocked to his door.

Priessnitz's treatment included a strict diet of simple food, mainly bread, milk and potatoes. Alcohol and stimulants such as mustard and pepper were prohibited, as were warm beverages of any sort. All medicines, too, were *verboten*. The patient was expected to take light exercise, such as walking in the open air. The water cure itself involved drinking anything from five to forty tumblers in the course of a day. Patients also found themselves draped in wet blankets for three-hour periods (during which time they drank water through a tube); they then took a cold bath and sometimes received a rubdown. An *Umschlag*, or compress, a cloth wetted with cold water, was placed on the afflicted part of the body. Depending on the condition, the patient might also be given a sitz bath, a shower or a head bath. Although known primarily for using cold water in his cures, Priessnitz also put some of his patients in vapour baths.

Priessnitz's hydrotherapy attracted criticism from sceptical medical professionals, who called him a quack and a charlatan, but his popularity and reputation continued to spread. In 1826, when his fame had reached Vienna, he was asked to treat Anton Victor, Grand Master of the Teutonic Knights and brother of Francis II, the

Holy Roman Emperor. In 1838 he was granted permission to build a spa, and in 1843 the *New England Journal of Medicine* reported that he had under his care an archduchess, ten princes and princesses, at least a hundred counts and barons, as well as numerous military men, lawyers, professors and even a number of physicians.[1] In that same year his treatise on hydrotherapy appeared in an English edition, entitled *The Cold Water Cure, its Principles, Theory, and Practice, with Ample Directions for its Self-Application, and a Full Account of the Wonderful Cures Performed with it on 7,000 Patients of All Nations.*

THREE WEEKS IN WET SHEETS

The water cure soon came to England thanks to Priessnitz's enthusiastic patients and disciples. Richard Claridge, a captain in the Middlesex Militia who had spent time in Gräfenberg, published his account of Priessnitz's treatments and techniques in January 1842 as *Hydropathy; or The Cold Water Cure, as practiced by Vincent Priessnitz*; afterwards he founded a number of societies for promoting the cure. By the time Claridge's work appeared in print, two hydrotherapy centre were already operating in England – one at Stansteadbury in Hertfordshire, under the direction of a German named Joseph Weiss, and another at Ham in Surrey, likewise run by a German doctor, a Bavarian named von Schlemmer, who soon afterwards moved to Stansteadbury before, late in 1842, moving to Ewell, near Epsom, with the plan of founding a hydropathic college.

It was in the Malvern Hills, however, rather than in Surrey or Hertfordshire, that hydrotherapy would be promoted and practised most vigorously. The man responsible for publicizing the merits of hydrotherapy in England was Dr James Wilson. He spent a year at Priessnitz's clinic in Gräfenberg as both a patient and then an enthusiastic student before returning to London in 1842 at the age of 35 'filled to the brim', as a friend and colleague later claimed, with Priessnitz's ideas about hydrotherapy (quite literally: at

Gräfenberg he once downed thirty flasks of water before breakfast).[2] Wilson was well qualified as a doctor, having studied medicine at Dublin, London and Paris. His medical practice in Piccadilly was next door to his fellow doctor, James Manby Gully, whose wealthy family owned a coffee plantation in Jamaica. Gully was equally well qualified as a medical practitioner, possessing medical qualifications from Liverpool, Edinburgh and Paris. Wilson persuaded Gully to join forces with him and in establishing a hydrotherapy centre. Gully was easily converted to the cause, convinced as he was that conventional medicine was 'effete, inefficient, if not positively harmful'[3] – an opinion possibly reached following the successive deaths of his wife from smallpox and youngest daughter from croup.

Searching for an appropriate location to set up their new business, the two physicians settled on Malvern, an old spa town with seventy springs and other water sources. Elizabeth I had granted John Hornyold the land with its numerous medicinal wells in 1558. From 1622 the water from the Holy Well and the Eye Well (known as such for curing eye diseases) were both drunk at the site and bottled and sold. The commercial reach of these bottled waters is suggested in an old Malvern song from the mid-eighteenth century:

A thousand bottles there,
Were filled weekly,
And many costrils rare,
For stomachs sickly;
Some of them into Kent,
Some were to London sent,
Others to Berwick went,
   O praise the Lord.[4]

The four most popular springs in Malvern were Holy Well, the Eye Well, Hay Well and – at 850 feet above sea level and a steep walk from the town – St Ann's Well.[5] The waters of Malvern contain no minerals but had successfully been advertised by Dr

St Ann's Well, Malvern, depicted on a postcard. Those reaching this elevated site either climbed or availed themselves of a donkey.

John Wall in the mid-seventeenth century as therapeutically pure and possessing great qualities if drunk fresh, on the spot, and at regular intervals. The absence of mineral content was trumpeted as a virtue. When Dr Wall tested Malvern water in 1757 he concluded that its efficacy 'seems chiefly to arise from its great purity'.[6] This opinion gave rise to the popular ditty: 'The Malvern water is famous for containing just nothing at all.' Yet this lack of mineral content did not mean it was ineffective; quite the contrary. Dr Wall went on to describe countless cases of people who benefited from Malvern's waters, such as a 26-year-old man cured of the King's Evil and woman with a 'scrofulous' eye who, following one week of treatment, 'could see a Flea leaping on her Bed'. He believed that

An advertisement for 'Malvernia', a sparkling drink made from Malvern's 'exquisitely pure' waters, c.1900.

Malvern's waters could cure even the most dreadful of diseases, since in the case of a woman from Powick the waters, taken both internally and externally, cleared 'the most frightful Leprosy I ever saw'.[7] We may doubt whether Malvern waters cure leprosy, but modern studies do indeed show that it contains no minerals or bacteria, and that it has the purity of distilled water. For this reason it has been awarded EU status as natural spring water.

In 1757 Wall built a bathhouse at the Holy Well and lodgings named Wells House were added.[8] By 1800 Malvern was already a popular tourist destination for wealthy invalids and those seeking fresh air. The botanist Benjamin Stillingfleet wrote to Elizabeth Montagu in 1757, praising the waters and noting that the hike necessary to drink them may have been a factor in the town's reputation for restoring people to health: 'I do not doubt but that the air and exercise, which at present is absolutely necessary here, the well being about two miles from the town, contribute very much towards restoring the health of the patients.'[9] In 1831 a Malvern doctor named William Addison, physician to the Duchess of Kent, wrote how Malvern was 'annually becoming more and more the resort of visitors and invalids seeking health or protection from disease'.[10] Londoners could reach the resort in a day and a half, catching the Hereford mail coach at the White Horse Cellar in Piccadilly at 8:30 a.m. and arriving in Malvern at 3 p.m. on the following day. The town's credentials were burnished when 12-year-old Princess Victoria visited on a tour in 1830 that also included Leamington Spa and Bath.

Malvern's geographical location was perfect for Wilson and Gully. The Malvern Hills surrounding the town provided clean, bracing air, and the opportunity for brisk hilly walks – essential to their healing regime (although the more infirm could ride donkeys up the hills and to the wells). Wilson, who moved to the town in 1842, arrived a few months before Gully. He first stayed at the Crown Hotel and after buying the hostelry and renaming it Gräfenberg House – a homage to Priessnitz – he opened his hydrotherapy centre. In the first two years, he wrote two books on the water cure, demand for which became so great that he commissioned larger premises, completed eight years later, in nearby Abbey Road. This new establishment, boasting rooms for fifty guests, was christened Priessnitz House, once again in tribute to his hero. A medical consultation cost 1 guinea, while 4 guineas a week provided four supervised baths, with an additional expense for a private sitting room or servants' quarters.

Following his own move to Malvern, Dr Gully eventually practised out of two rival establishments: Tudor House for men, and Holyrood House for women, with the houses linked by a bridge known as the 'Bridge of Sighs'. For ten years these two doctors were the only hydrotherapy practitioners in Malvern, but as the popularity of their treatments spread, more doctors, apothecaries, builders and traders arrived, turning Malvern into the kind of prosperous and fashionable spa town about which, many decades earlier, Dr Wall had dreamed. Gully treated such distinguished patients as Alfred Lord Tennyson, Thomas Carlyle, Bishop Samuel Wilberforce and Charles Darwin. The last arrived in Malvern in 1849, suffering from a constellation of alarming and debilitating symptoms – palpitations, vomiting, headaches, dizziness, trembling hands, skin problems, flatulence – the causes of which are still debated. Gully put him on a strict diet and gave him a gruelling regimen.

Darwin described the routine in a letter to his sister Susan. He rose at 6:45 a.m. to be greeted by a washerman and 'scrubbed with rough towel in cold water for 2 or 3 minutes', which made him look, he said, 'very like a lobster'. He then drank a tumbler of water, dressed, and walked for twenty minutes. His breakfast consisted of toast with meat or egg, along with – as per Darwin's request – milk in which to sop the toast (his only luxury apart from six daily pinches of snuff). 'At no time must I take any sugar, butter, spices tea bacon or anything good', he lamented. Throughout the day he was compelled to wear a compress, which he described as 'a broad wet folded linen covered by mackintosh & which is "refreshed" – ie dipt in cold water every 2 hours ... I don't perceive much effect from this of any kind.' At noon his feet went into a bucket of cold water for ten minutes, after which they were 'violently rubbed' by the washerman. Then came another twenty-minute walk, followed at one o'clock by a meal of plum pudding and then a short nap. Next came another cold-water bath for the feet, followed by second twenty-minute walk. 'Supper same as breakfast.' He still felt much sickness, he reported to Susan, but his feet were warmer and his spirits higher. On the following day he was to be wrapped for an hour in a wet blanket with a hot bottle to his feet, then rubbed with a 'cold dripping sheet'.[11]

Darwin persisted with the harsh regime of the water cure following his return to Down House in Kent, even having a cold-water shower built. He returned to Malvern in 1851 when his beloved 10-year-old daughter Annie fell seriously ill. To his tremendous grief she died in the town, after which he laid her to rest in the churchyard of Great Malvern Priory.

Two years after Darwin's 1849 stay, a journalist named Joseph Leech wrote an amusing account of his own experience of the Malvern water cure, in his case at one of Dr Wilson's establishments. He called it *Three Weeks in Wet Sheets, being the diary and doings of A Moist Visitor to Malvern.*[12] He stayed at Priessnitz House, which had 'an air of massive repose' enhanced by many of the patients, ladies and gentlemen, promenading the gardens, albeit watched through the railing by townspeople 'with much the same curiosity and commiseration they might be expected to bestow upon the inmates of Hanwell Lunatic Asylum'.[13]

Leech arrived for his first appointment with Dr Sturmes, a colleague of Wilson's, and learned that for the last ten years he had been 'committing slow but deliberate suicide' by enjoying good dinners.[14] Diet, Leech soon realized, was an essential part of the water cure. Breakfast consisted of nothing but bread and treacle, with absolutely no reviving morning cup of tea. Doctors carefully weighed out how much bread each individual could eat. 'It was amusing', Leech observed, 'to see them snip off a bit here or add a bit there until they had precisely fixed the prescribed 4 oz, which was the standard of health.' The noon meal was no better: mutton and vegetables, followed by rice pudding, semolina or tapioca for dessert. For afternoon tea, more of the same: more bread, lots of butter (denied to Darwin) and gooey treacle, with the staff exercising a 'salutary surveillance' over the inmates that reminded Leech of the

First morning at the Water Cure.
(Bathman brings the Wet sheet.)
"But I am sure I shall get my death
of cold."

Sitz Bath & Wet sheet 6 o'clock winter's morn't.
"This is delightful, very !!!"

Illustrations from *Pleasures of the Water Cure* by Thomas Onwhyn, 1860, showing water treatments such as the 'rain bath' the 'douche' and wrapping in wet sheets.

attentions of the Paris police. This spartan diet soon found Leech gazing wistfully into confectioners' shops, eyeing the cheesecakes in the windows.

The water treatments themselves caused Leech astonishment, unease and, occasionally, exhilaration. In his bedroom, two baths were positioned opposite each other: an ordinary tub as well as a hip bath. 'I had barely time to undress, and was not allowed leisure to feel nervous, when the executioner – I mean my bath-man – appeared, a good-humoured looking fellow, about thirty, with a wet sheet slightly wrung out of the cold water in his hand, and this he abruptly popped over my head and body.' The wet sheet in contact with his body supposedly stimulated and refreshed him as the bath-man 'rubbed lustily away'. Leech was left feeling an invisible glow of heat. The bath-man insisted the spray from the wet sheet was as precious as a 'shower of pearls'.[15]

THE PACKING.
"Don't I look very like a Mummy."

THE PACKING
"Now this is what I call being jolly."

Over the next three weeks, Leech experienced many different water treatments with mixtures of amusement and horror. For the Lamp Bath his bath-man placed a wooden frame around the chair and spread blankets over the frame until they reached his chin, creating a marquee or tent of sorts, while his feet rested on a footstool. A lamp was placed under his chair, with the wooden frame barely stopping the blankets from catching alight. The bath-man assured Leech that he only knew of two cases of ignition – neither at Priessnitz House. Hardly reassured, Leech sweated, dripping excessively from his forehead and nose; he 'began to think of Ridley and Cranmer, and a martyrdom in singed blankets'. After ten minutes the bath-man removed the blankets and instructed Leech to jump briskly into the cold bath awaiting for him. 'I did as I was bid, though at any other time I should have thought it deliberate suicide – madness itself – an act of insane self-destruction.' Just as

THE RAIN BATH.

"You must be shut in for 15 minutes Sir!"

THE DOUCHE.

"Oh! Oh! Oh! Oh!"

Leech was getting used to the shock of the cold water, the bath-man poured six gallons of cold water over his head. Teeth chattering, Leech was removed from the bath, dried with a sheet and wrapped in a blanket; then his feet were rubbed, after which he was told to dress and go for a walk. He obliged the bath-man, amazed that he felt 'as brisk as a bee, and as light as a fairy'.

Brisk walks were an essential daily event, and patients regularly marched around the town carrying 'Gräfenberg tumblers' – vessels from which to drink the waters – and clutching Malvern Staffs, 6-foot-long ash walking sticks that made hill-climbing easier. Leech reported resting at the little house at St Ann's Well on his way to the Beacon – not to sample the waters or listen to the German band from Wiesbaden that entertained resting patients, but rather because he had heard that some enterprising soul was grilling calf kidneys for surreptitious consumption by hungry patients.

Leech was to try all the water treatments during his three-week stay, including body packing. On that occasion, the bath-man burst into his room and instructed him to rise from his bed, which was quickly stripped of its sheets. Five blankets were laid on the mattress in succession and then covered with a wet sheet. Leech was instructed to lie on top of these layers, recounting 'what a chill it sent through my frame as the fellow wrapped it round my warm body'. The bath-man cocooned him in all six blankets, leaving him in a 'cold misery' and feeling like a mummy wrapped in damp papyrus. But the heat of his body gradually began to conquer the wet sheet and he felt 'deliciously warm'. After fifty minutes, during which time Leech fell asleep, the bath-man unwrapped him and told him to jump into the cold water bath, where another 6 gallons of cold water anointed his head.

Leech also experienced a douche bath, which involved having cold water from a pipe pour onto his head from a height of 20 feet, causing him to cry out 'in terror and rapture'. After ninety seconds of this aquatic pummelling – which at one point knocked him off his feet – he dashed to the dressing room where the bath-man wrapped him in a dry sheet. It proved to be his favourite treatment, as 'it stimulates, it invigorates, it warms', giving him the power, he claimed, to jump over the moon or singlehandedly conquer a thousand men.

Getting wrapped in damp sheets may not have been the most pleasant experience on offer at a spa. Yet recent research indicates that this treatment may well have done good for at least some of those 'moist visitors'. Wet-wrap therapy has been shown to have positive effects on combatting obesity, in treating children with atopic dermatitis, and in conditions as wide-ranging as dyspepsia, diabetes, nervous disorders, general paresis, delirium tremens and fever. Wet-sheet-pack therapy has even been used successfully in helping caregivers deal with severe aggressive behaviours in children and adolescents hospitalized in psychiatric settings.[16]

By 1850 at least twenty water-cure establishments had opened in Britain, in places such as Dunstable, Manchester, Grasmere, Aberdeen, the Isle of Man, Ryde on the Isle of Wight, and Rothesay on the Isle of Bute. Ramsgate and Cheltenham each offered two. This proliferation continued despite the fact that the water cure was implicated in a number of deaths within a few years of its introduction to England. A patient treated for gout at Stansteadbury, Sir Francis Burdett, a prominent reformist politician, died at his London home in January 1844. *The Times* quoted reports that Sir Francis had been 'a victim to what is termed the hydropathic system of treatment', that he had taken to riding around London wrapped in wet towels, and that his daughter declared that 'the cold water treatment had destroyed one of the noblest constitutions ever given to man'.[17]

Even worse publicity followed two years later. In 1846 another practitioner, Dr James Ellis of Sudbrook Park in Petersham, Surrey, was charged with the manslaughter of a patient, a 45-year-old London accountant named Richard Dresser. The charge read that he had 'injuriously, rashly, negligently, and feloniously caused certain cloths, saturated with water, to be placed upon the body of the said Richard Dresser for a long period of time', that he had placed him in a bath of cold water, and that 'by these means he caused him to be mortally disordered in his body' such that he died of a congestion of the heart and lungs.[18] A coroner's inquest found Dr Ellis guilty, but two weeks later, at the Central Criminal Court, he was found not guilty and discharged. Charles Darwin clearly had enough confidence in the establishment: still seeking a cure for his mysterious afflictions, he visited Sudbrook in 1860.

Death and scandal continued to haunt hydrotherapy — quite sensationally in the case of James Gully. He and Wilson were very different in both their approaches and their personalities, and it was only a few years before, perhaps inevitably, they fell out. Gully was a confident and popular speaker, an advocate for women's suffrage and homeopathy, and he was not above using diagnostic clairvoyance and mesmerism to assist in his diagnoses. He boasted of treating his well-known celebrities – Darwin, Bishop Wilberforce and the others. Wilson, on the other hand, was a private, serious personality, who took a more traditional approach. While Wilson concentrated on his medical treatments, Gully engaged himself in developing Malvern as a resort. With his extroverted personality he put himself forward as chairman of the Malvern Improvement Commission, founded the *Malvern News* and became involved in the construction of a new railway station, a new school (Malvern College), a gas works and a luxury hotel.

After Wilson died in 1867, Gully continued to practise for a further five years before handing his business over to his partner, Dr W.T. Fernie. All did not end well for Gully, however, for he became involved in one of the great murder mysteries of Victorian London. At the age of 70, with his wife still alive and well in Brighton, he fell in love with a young widow named Florence Ricardo. They kept their affair secret, and he allegedly performed an abortion on her after impregnating her during a trip to the Continent to study hydrotherapy. Although they remained friends, Florence married the lawyer Charles Delauney Bravo in 1875 and moved into a grand home, The Priory, in Balham, South London, just down the road from where Gully was living at Orwell Lodge in Bedford Hill Road. When Bravo succumbed to antimony poisoning in April 1876, both Gully and Florence were obvious suspects. Two inquests were held, the first returning an open verdict, the second one of wilful murder. No one was ever charged, and nothing could be proved against Gully, but his reputation suffered from the publicity. He withdrew from public life, alienated and embittered, dying at Orwell Lodge in 1883.

About the same time Wilson and Gully set up hydrotherapy centres in Malvern, another convert from the Gräfenberg hydrotherapy centre in Silesia decided to do something similar in Ilkley, West Yorkshire. The former mayor of Leeds, Hamer Stansfield, persuaded friends to create a consortium to build the Wharfedale Hydropathic Establishment and Ben Rhydding Hotel.

Ilkley already had cold-water baths – three of them, in fact. Ilkley had an ancient well reputedly good for treating scrofulous cases when the water was either drunk or bathed in. In 1760 the local landowners, the Middeltons, constructed three baths, the establishment ultimately known as White Wells, high above the town – cold-water plunge baths that, high on the moor, were not for the fainthearted. A roof was not added until the 1820s and merely setting out 'on Ilkla Moor baht 'at' (without a hat) – as the Yorkshire song reminds us – could make a person 'catch thy deeath o' cowd'. Reaching White Wells was not an endeavour for the frail and infirm in any weather, even on a donkey (as people often did) following the craggy, winding path. Stansfield could see the advantages of the pure, cold waters but realized that to become successful his establishment needed to be more accessible.

Ben Rhydding Hydro was therefore built on Otley in Wharfedale, on the edge of Ilkley Moor. Stansfield designed the house with turrets, giving it the appearance of a grandiose castle. Rooms were luxurious, with private bathrooms and entertainments that included a bowling alley. When its doors opened in 1844, treatment followed a similar format to those in Gräfenberg and Malvern: wet sheets, cold showers, bracing hill walks, and a plain diet with the added bonus of hearing the Scriptures read aloud each day after breakfast.

In 1847 Dr William Macleod, after spending time in Malvern with Wilson and Gully, became manager of the Ben Rhydding Hydro. Macleod saw a tempting business opportunity and soon

Ben Rhydding Hydro, built in Wharfedale, on the edge of Ilkley Moor. Transfer lithograph by J.R. Jobbins (active 1839-64) after C. Brodrick.

bought all the shares, at which point he began making substantial changes, including adding a Turkish bath and creating three separate baths based on his interpretation of an Ancient Roman bath. The first room he called the *frigidarium*, an open-topped room with couches and dressing rooms to prepare clients for their Turkish bath and then for relaxation afterwards. The next room, the *tepidarium*, was a smaller room with steamy temperatures of 32–34°C (90–110°F), followed by the hottest bath, the *calidarium*, where temperatures reached 60–65°C (140–150°F). Macleod decided against incorporating the rough Turkish massage, introducing instead a gentler version on shampooing tables ('shampoo' comes from the Hindustani word for kneading, pressing or massaging). Cold-water baths were naturally provided, as well as douches, with men and women allotted separate days for their treatments. Unlike in Malvern, under Macleod's management at the Ben Rhydding plenty of fine food and alcohol was available.

The beauty of Ilkley and the Victorian enthusiasm for the water cure soon attracted other entrepreneurs to the area. In 1856 Benjamin Briggs Popplewell and a group of Bradford businessmen bought land on the southern slopes of Ilkley Moor to build the Wells House Hydro. It was initially run by a German, a Dr Antoin Rischanek, but his 'foreign ways' proved unpopular in Yorkshire, and before long he was replaced by a Sheffield doctor.[19] Within a few years, another establishment opened nearby, Craiglands, whose name referred to Craig Tor on the adjoining moor. Various other establishments likewise opened in the second half of the century, such as Rockwood House, Marlborough House and Moorlands. All offered the comforts of a high-class vacation with the damp sheets of the water cure.

The increased competition, both in Ilkley and from elsewhere, caused a drop in patient numbers at Ben Rhydding. The addition of a golf course in 1890 failed to attract more patients, but when golf ultimately proved more popular than hydrotherapy the spa became the Ben Rhydding Golf Hotel. During the Second World War the hotel was recommissioned for the Wool Control Board and in 1955, having never reopened as a hotel, the building was demolished.

QUACKING WITH JOY

The Ben Rhydding Hydro was responsible for spawning a similar treatment centre in Matlock, Derbyshire. In 1846 a wealthy 43-year-old cotton-mill owner named John Smedley contracted a chill and a fever while on honeymoon in Switzerland. Years of treatment with drugs proved ineffective (one alarming manifestation of his illness was a religious mania). Then in 1849 he spent time wrapped in damp sheets in Ilkley. Smedley was so impressed with the water cure that he dedicated the rest of his life to establishing a hydrotherapy hospital for his employees at Lea Mills. Since many working people could not afford the fees most hydrotherapy centres charged for a month's treatment, Smedley had patients from his mill treated at his house, which he turned into a free hospital. The Smedley Hydro had its origins in the small dwelling that he purchased on the Matlock Bank in order to house six patients, who paid 6 shillings per day. It opened in 1853, and Smedley continued to treat patients for free in his home. Recognizing that not all patients, especially the frail, could withstand the harsh regime and frigid waters applied in Gräfenberg, Malvern and Ilkley, Smedley adjusted the temperature of the waters to spare the most delicate frames. He also treated his patients with mustard packs – an innovation the purists saw as a departure from the water cure, and one that, moreover, had been introduced by a layman, they argued, rather than a physician. 'Yes,' wrote one of his defenders, 'because John Smedley had not got a series of letters tailing off after his name he was a quack. Anyway he quacked to good purpose, and sent his patients away quacking with joy over their restored good health!'[20]

Matlock, in a gorge alongside the River Derwent, had been developed as a spa in the early decades of the eighteenth century, complete with baths, hotels and an assembly room. It was in the latter establishment in 1804 that the bashful young Lord Byron, a Harrow schoolboy unable to dance because of his club foot, watched in envy as his cousin Mary Chaworth was led onto the floor. By that time Matlock had become a fashionable watering hole. Smedley's was not the first hydro in the area; three others had opened in previous years, including the one in Darley Dale, 2 miles distant, opened by Dr Rischanek in 1848 following his departure from Ben Rhydding. His house featured fourteen bedrooms, a beautiful dining room, pleasure gardens, baths, douches and accommodation for twenty patients. However, Smedley's Hydro became the most well known in Derbyshire, in part due to its owner's forceful personality and missionary zeal. God played an essential role in his personal life as well as in the water treatments. In 1850, having fallen out with the Church of England and converted to Free Methodism, he built a number of schools and chapels around Matlock, earning the nickname the 'Prophet of the Peaks' – a moniker that owed as much to his faith in water as to his faith in God.

Daily routine at Smedley's establishment was regimented, disciplined and frugal. He claimed that his system of treatment was mild, 'with the application of bandages, not used in the same way elsewhere, and some newly invented baths'.[21] Meals were simple, while books, newspapers, tobacco and alcohol were banned. Visitors were banned on Sundays. The establishment had a monastic element, complete with periodic silences and readings from the Scriptures. Fines were levied on anyone who broke the rules. The effectiveness of his treatments meant patient numbers steadily increased. In 1860, 110 patients visited Smedley's, with numbers three years later climbing to 1,050, plus more than 400 more treated at his free hospital. By 1867, some 2,000 patients visited each institution.[22] So many new patients wished to attend that in 1868 Smedley was obliged to add a new four-storey wing.

Smedley died in 1874, but not without having groomed a successor, a young doctor named William Bell Hunter. A limited company purchased the Hydro and improvements were made to the house. Dr Bell Hunter remained in post until his death in 1894. Smedley's wife Caroline Ann lived for more than twenty years after her husband's death, opening the Smedley Memorial Hydropathic Hospital on Bank Road in 1882 as a memorial to her husband. This was not part of the new Smedley company and relied on subscribers to continue its role as a hospital for the poor.

In 1891 *Kelly's Derbyshire Trades Directory* listed more than twenty hydropathic centres in Matlock. By that time, however, the water cure had spread far beyond Malvern, Ilkley and Matlock, having reached all parts of the United Kingdom. As early as the 1860s more than twenty new treatment centres had appeared in established spa towns as original bathhouses were converted for hydrotherapy or else purpose-built facilities were attached to hotels. Hospitals that offered free spa treatments to the poor – the Bath Mineral Hospital, the Devonshire Royal Hospital in Buxton and Margate's Royal Sea Bathing Hospital – all added the latest hydropathic services and equipment to their treatments.

NINE

A Lot of Hot Air

VAPOUR PUMPS AND TURKISH BATHS

In the first years of the nineteenth century there was a lot of hot air in Downing Street. 'Under the Patronage of the Royal Family', an advertisement printed in *The Times* read in 1813. It touted the benefits of a 'Turkish Medicated Vapour-bath' whose premises were to be found at 3 Downing Street. Its proprietor assured the newspaper's readers that this bath, constructed on 'the Turkish plan', was the only one of its kind in the country. 'It has already been patronised by several distinguished Noblemen, Ladies and Gentlemen of distinction', the advertisement declared. It supposedly proved a safe and efficacious remedy for the usual medical suspects – scorbutic and scrofulous conditions, gout, rheumatism, stone and gravel, and so forth. 'Due attention is paid to adapt the accommodations to the sex and rank of the patient', readers were assured, and the bath was available not merely for the sick but to anyone who wished to use it for 'luxurious enjoyment'.[1]

For anyone who found the frigid water and harsh regime of hydrotherapy unappealing, other options existed in the first half of the nineteenth century – ones such as this Downing Street

The Turkish Baths in Harrogate.

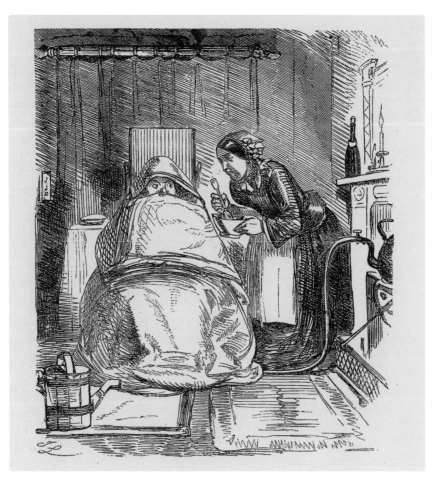

In Victorian times, patients could book a practitioner to give them a steam bath at home. Undated wood engraving.

Turkish bath that made use of hot air and medicated vapours. In Victorian Britain, enthusiasm for vapour treatments and Turkish baths developed in tandem with that for hydrotherapy. A number of enterprising practitioners even offered home services, from medicated vapours and steam baths to immersion in warm sulphurous waters in tubs brought into the patient's house at a moment's notice. If many people in Britain once believed that steam baths were confined to 'the wild Irish, the Red Indian, the cruel Turk, or the enslaved Russian', the mania for sitting and sweating half-naked in scorching temperatures and then submitting to vigorous rubdowns eventually captured the enthusiasm of the upright and uptight Victorians.

I GOT S-S-S-STEAM HEAT

The practice of using vapours to treat patients appears to have originated with an Italian, a Venetian immigrant to London named Dr Bartholomew de Dominicetti. In 1765 Dominichetti opened a heated and medicated water bath in Cheyne Walk in London. The baths included unique vapour pumps and dry baths that applied moisture to the whole body. Dominicetti claimed his baths cured a wide range of diseases, including leprosy, scurvy, dropsies, ulcers, as well as tumours of the womb, urethra, bladder and breast. One sceptic was Samuel Johnson, who claimed in conversation with friends: 'There is nothing in all this boasted system.' When one of Johnson's friends protested that medicines of various sorts could, in fact, be introduced through the pores into the human body by means of steam and warm water, Johnson retorted: 'Well, sir, go to Dominicetti and get thyself fumigated; but be sure that the steam be directed to thy head, for that is the peccant part.' As James Boswell reported: 'This produced a triumphant roar of laughter from the motley assembly of philosophers, printers, and dependents, male and female.'[2]

Despite allegedly having over 16,000 people on his books, including Edward, the Duke of York, Dominicetti still went bankrupt in 1782. His son Rodomonte, also a doctor, moved the remnants of his father's business to Flitwick in Bedfordshire, near to Ampthill, where his wife had been born. Leasing an imposing house and using his father's patented invention, the vapour apparatus, he continued in business for a further twenty years until in 1806, running into financial difficulties, he was forced to sell up and abandon Flitwick.

The principle of treating patients with steam and hot air continued through the first half of the nineteenth century thanks to the efforts of an entrepreneur named Michael La Beaume and his Air-Pump Vapour-Bath. This device was a portable sudatory – a contraption taken door to door to make the patient sweat. La Beaume was a great believer in the benefits of perspiration, which freed the body from 'acrid and impure humours'.[3] He maintained that most diseases were caused by 'checked perspiration or the unhealthy state of the skin' – the skin being, he noted, the body's largest organ, with one grain of sand covering 125,000 pores. Checked perspiration led to all number of diseases and complaints, and the key to recovery and good health was its restoration through the application of warm vapours. A hot bath could do the trick, he allowed, but the trouble of procuring a tin bath, of conveying it into the sick room, of heating and regulating the temperature of the water, of removing the invalid from bed and helping him or her into the water – such logistics, he argued, served to counterbalance the good effects of a steamy bath.

Hence the Air-Pump Vapour-Bath, which was invented, La Beaume noted, by a Mr Smith of Brighton, although it may have owed something in concept or design to Dominicetti's vapour pump. Inspired by the technique of sucking poison from wounds, Smith had decided to find a mechanical means to give the body a much more powerful and efficacious purge. Smith seems never to have deployed it, but by 1819 La Beaume had begun using it to treat numerous diseases and conditions. He consulted from his home in Southampton Row each day between noon and 4 p.m., except Sundays. By the 1820s he often received frantic summonses from physicians to make house calls to treat their patients, since, as a lightweight contraption, it could be taken into the patient's lodgings.

An elaborately dressed woman pampers a man in a vapour-bath. Coloured etching after Godissart de Cari, c. 1820.

It consisted of a metal and wickerwork cylinder in which the patient (or the afflicted limb) was encased, a spirit lamp that heated water in a small boiler, a tube that conducted the steam into the cylinder, a thermometer that gave the temperature of the fumigation, and stopcocks to regulate the flow of air. Medications could even be added to the vapours. The patient would soon feel 'a genial glow, first in the feet, and thence ascending to the bowels', and then in the rest of the body – stomach, chest, extremities and head – as healthy perspiration was restored.[4]

La Beaume, who called himself a 'medical surgical electrician',[5] was committed applying the latest scientific advances to disease.

Excited about the possibilities for curing patients with electrical stimulation as well as steam, he sometimes, if the situation called for it, added galvanism to the treatment. He followed the theories of Luigi Galvani, the Italian scientist who investigated the effect of electricity on animals, and whose nephew Giovanni Aldini demonstrated, at Newgate Prison in 1803, the effects of electrical stimulation – a twitching jaw and contorted limbs – on the corpse of an executed criminal. At his home in London, La Beaume experimented with Aldini's equipment, giving himself electrical shocks to find the right amount of stimulus for his patients. Ultimately he committed himself to galvanism rather than steam, becoming (as he proudly advertised) 'Galvanist and Electrician to the Queen'.[6] Like the Dominichettis, however, he suffered financial reversals, and in 1847 he appeared in court for bankruptcy, owing £1,186 to 139 different creditors.[7]

The benefits of curing disease through vapour baths were explored and promoted by a number of other doctors and entrepreneurs in the first decades of the nineteenth century. In 1820 a Dr Green began operating 'fumigating and vapour baths' in Great Marlborough Street in London, submerging his patients in the hot waters of his fumigating box. In the same year Mr Whitlaw's Vapour Bath Establishment opened in Finsbury Park. Charles Whitlaw was a botanist who had travelled extensively in North America and the West Indies, experimenting with new ways of packing and preserving plants for use in both food and medicine. During the course of his travels he encountered the sweat lodges of the Native Americans, witnessing how water was sprinkled on heated stones placed inside a tent 'while the patients sat around the stones, until perspiration was produced'.[8] Struck by the benefits, he decided to administer plant-based medications in similar fashion, treating patients in London with his vapour baths before arriving in New York in 1824. Despite encountering hostility from many medical professionals, he set up

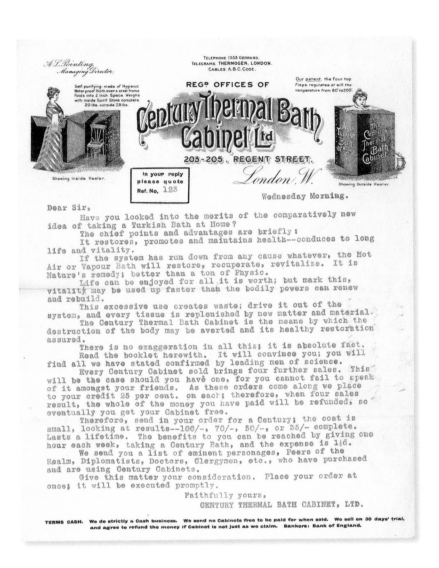

A late-nineteenth-century advertisement for a Century Thermal Bath Cabinet for the home, featuring a waterproof cloth and a spirit stove.

vapour bath companies throughout the country and persuaded fifty doctors of its benefits.

When he then returned to London in 1825, Whitlaw began offering his medicated vapour baths as a way of promoting perspiration in order to treat skin diseases, asthma, digestive disorders,

quinsy, measles, whooping cough, gout and even hydrophobia.
He also maintained that perspiration could remove mercury and
lead from the body. During the epidemic of 1831–2 both he and
La Beaume expressed optimism that their baths would help treat
cholera. After opening new premises in Regent Street, Whitlaw
raised funds for a Medicated Vapour Bath Institution 'for the benefit
of the operative mechanics, domestic and other servants, and sick
poor'.[9] It opened in Great Castle Street, near Oxford Circus,
accepting male patients for treatment on Tuesdays and Fridays,
female patients on Mondays and Thursdays.

Competition in the medical bathing industry in London grew intense. A physician named Robert Culverwell opened his home in North London to bathers in the late 1820s, posting a signboard reading 'WARM BATHS' and immersing patients in a lead-lined wooden bath. One day he treated so many of them that the copper chimney used to heat the water caught fire, requiring the urgent

MERTON STREET BATHS.

Turkish, Tepid Swimming & Hot Baths,
MERTON STREET, OXFORD.

Proprietor :—FREDK. DOLLEY.

THESE BATHS, having been remodelled and refurnished with all modern improvements, now combine, under one roof and one management, the most complete arrangement for the convenience and comfort of all patrons of the Bath.

The Turkish Bath is heated by a continuous circulation of pure hot air and ventilated on the most improved principle.

The Rooms have been refurnished throughout, and the Cooling Room supplied with Daily Papers, Magazines, &c. Choice Cigars, Coffee, and other refreshments supplied on reasonable terms.

The Tepid Swimming Bath, 70 ft. long by 30 ft. wide, and varying in depth from 4 to 6 feet, will be kept at a temperature of 70° Fahr.

Swimming taught by an experienced Professor.

The Private Hot Baths are supplied with a Hot and Cold Shower, which can be modulated at will, thus effectually preventing any taking cold from the use of the hot bath alone.

SWIMMING LESSONS.

14 Lessons (payable in advance)   £1 5 0
Special terms for schools and Families.
Lessons can be given at any time of the year, the bath
being kept at a temperature of 70° Fahr.

Advertisement for Merton Street Baths, c1885–90.

summoning of fire engines. 'The mania was in full force', he later wrote.[10] To meet the demand he eventually converted a stable and coach house in his rear garden into bath houses, and he later opened establishments in Lothbury, near the Bank of England, and then in New Bond Street, offering warm baths in sulphurous, medicated and Harrogate waters.

Other companies could provide a home service to invalids – not merely vapour baths like La Beaume's, but full immersion in a variety of different kinds of water. The Royal Portable-Bath Company operated out of an address at 71½ Oxford Street. Here, by the early 1840s, its 'commodious establishment' offered bathing rooms that were 'the most replete in the metropolis'. Yet it also took its baths abroad: for a cost of 8 shillings it sent out warm baths to private houses, especially for the treatment of the sick. The warm bath could be provided at a few minutes' notice, the company claimed, at any time of the day or night. It provided not only medicated vapour baths but also a remarkable range that included warm or tepid water, as well as sulphur, seawater and water from Harrogate. Warm bathing linen was also supplied.[11]

The Royal Portable-Bath Company soon went out of business. But devotees of hot baths would soon have another way of taking the waters.

'AS IN TURKEY'

The two Victorian methods of taking the waters, hydrotherapy and steam baths, overlapped in the person of an Irish country doctor named Richard Barter. Born in County Cork in 1802, Barter became interested in treating patients with water during the cholera epidemic, publishing *On the Prevention and Cure of Cholera* in 1832. His enthusiasm for water cures only increased when, after his marriage, he moved to a small estate near Cork, St Anne's Hill, which included in its grounds an ancient holy well known as

St Anne's spring. Soon afterwards he met the Priessnitz disciple Captain Claridge, who was touring Ireland. Barter introduced hydropathy into Ireland, opening his establishment at St Anne's Hill in 1842 (soon after which the well ran dry, forcing him to hastily re-excavate). He offered treatments that included various douches and a novelty vapour (bath based on old Irish sweating houses), along with the customary hydrotherapy regime of cold baths, a rigorous diet and rural exertions. In 1856 he added hot water to his panoply of cures, opening a luxurious Turkish bath inspired by his reading of David Urquhart's 1850 travel memoir *The Pillars of Hercules*.

David Urquhart was the great exponent of Turkish baths in Britain. Born in 1805, he was an eccentric and charismatic Scottish diplomat and politician. He travelled extensively on the Continent before studying Classics at Oxford and then, inspired by Hellenism, taking part in the London Greek Committee's naval expedition to Greece in 1827. Wounded at the siege of Scio, he made his way to Constantinople and became part of a British diplomatic mission. Impressed with Turkish culture, he soon abandoned his Hellenism and went native, moving out of the embassy quarter and adopting Turkish clothing. In 1838 he published *The Spirit of the East*, a two-volume account of his decade in the East that celebrated Turkish society and praised Islam as close in dogma to the 'true Church'.[12] He even led a campaign to abolish the handshake in favour of performing Turkish salutations.

In keeping with his Turcophilia, back in England Urquhart spearheaded the Turkish Bath Movement, promoting Turkish baths as a means of providing cleansing facilities to working-class people with no access to running water. In 1856 he and Dr Barter

An 1871 advertisement for the Brighton Turkish Bath Company that extols the virtues of the 'hot-air Bath'.

THE BRIGHTON
TURKISH BATH COMPANY
(LIMITED)

TURKISH BATH,

(Established 1868, at a cost of £14,000,)

59, WEST STREET.

FOR GENTLEMEN.

from 8 a.m. to 8.30 p.m.

...	2s. each.
...	20s. per dozen.
...	3s. each.
...	30s. per dozen.

men *only*, from 8 o'clock a.m.

ETS 2s. EACH.

RS OF AGE, HALF-PRICE.

Bath may be weakening. But the
it be used improperly. The most
ity to destroy the sense of fatigue
at balance of nutrative functions of
gives us appetite and strengthens
body take up nutritive matter more

MR. ERASMUS WILSON.

liable every winter to attacks of
ct immunity from these complaints

DR. THUDICUM.

THE BRIGHTON
TURKISH BATH COMPANY
(LIMITED).

TURKISH BATH,

(Established 1868, at a cost of £14,000.)

59A, WEST STREET.

FOR LADIES.

The Bath is open from 8 o'clock a.m. till 8.30 p.m.

Private Bath	5s. each.
Series of Twelve ditto	50s.
Baths at any hour of the day	3s.
Series of Twelve	30s.
Ordinary Bath, from 5 p.m. to 8 p.m. ...	2s.
Series of Twelve	20s.

CHILDREN UNDER TWELVE YEARS OF AGE, HALF-PRICE.

The hot-air Bath is of great use in dyspeptic and gouty habits, and in those
who lead inactive lives.

SIR BENJAMIN BRODIE.

Throughout the East the *Hammam* is resorted to by all classes and ages of
both sexes as a thing of every day life, necessary for health and comfort.

DR. BRYCE.

What is it that makes the Turks such graceful and handsome men, and the
Turkish women so exquisitely lovely? Nothing in the world but their frequent
use of the bath.

DR. MILLIGAN.
5

collaborated on a treatise, *The Turkish Bath, with a View to its Introduction into the British Dominions*. Urquhart's interpretation of a Turkish bath differed from the original, known in the Ottoman Empire as a *hammam* (from the Arabic *hamma*, 'heating up'). Whereas a hammam heated water to create a steam bath – using much the same principle as a Scandinavian sauna or a North American sweat lodge – the English versions heated air with coal to produce a dry heat. A Victorian Turkish bath involved the bather making his or her way through a succession of chambers (some heated to a scorching 121°c, or 250°F), and then, after sweating profusely, plunging into cold water and receiving a massage and body wash. Urquhart regarded the Turkish bath as a more economical option than the traditional wash house or public bath since air was more plentiful and cheaper to heat than water. He also hoped his baths would break down barriers between the classes. 'No barrier of ceremony, of pride, or of habit, is so great', he wrote, 'as that of filth which, in these times, especially in large towns, separates the poor from the rich.'[13] Urquhart foresaw nothing less than a social reform in and through hygiene.

In 1857 Urquhart installed a Turkish bath in Riverside House, his family home on Money Hill Road in Rickmansworth. Open to the public, it consisted of two storeys, one in the basement, which were heated by a furnace. 'You leave your clothes in a little compartment below, and enter the bath on the basement story', Urquhart wrote. 'Here it is intended that you shall find the temperature as 100 degrees, and you find a cistern for plunging.' The bather then climbed the staircase to arrive at a platform where the heat reached 66°c (150°F), followed by another series of platforms leading to the ceiling where the temperature stood at 121°c (250°F). 'When your purification is accomplished,' he wrote, 'you robe yourself in a toga, and step out into a chamber looking out on the lawn and over the fields across the river.' Here, in this 'chamber of repose', the bather was treated to coffee, a hookah and various other refreshments, 'as in Turkey'.[14]

Urquhart's commitment to Turkish baths was to have tragic personal consequences. In February 1858 his 1-year-old son William died following treatment in the bath for convulsions suffered while teething. Scandal was then added to the tragedy. A coroner's inquest found the evidence regarding the cause of death unsatisfactory, but afterwards a jury member, a stationer and newsagent from Rickmansworth, gave an account to the *Buckingham Advertiser* claiming that the jury 'highly censured the treatment pursued towards the deceased', and that the child's body had been scarred and covered in blood. Neither of these allegations was true. The jury had actually found that Urquhuart and his wife Harriet always treated William with the greatest kindness, and that his older brother had received benefits from a similar treatment.[15]

A second death occurred later that same year. In the summer of 1858 *The Times* carried a gruesome headline: 'The Awful Death in a Hot-Air Bath'. It told the story of Joseph Smith, an 80-year-old who died in a Turkish bath in Honley in the West Riding of Yorkshire. The bath had been erected by 'an intelligent working man' named Joseph Laycock who 'has for some time interested himself in the subject of Turkish or hot-air baths'. Laycock allowed his friends and neighbours to use the bath, which adjoined his house, and Smith – 'a very eccentric, though harmless old man' – apparently received much benefit from it. One Monday afternoon he requested a bath from Mrs Laycock even though her husband was absent. Since Smith was 'remarkable for his stubbornness', Mrs Laycock finally agreed and heated the airtight tiled bath. Smith entered when the temperature reached 53°C (128°F), which a surgeon testified was the proper temperature for a man his age. He spent an hour and fifteen minutes inside, with Mrs Laycock checking on him several times. On her last check she heard a groan, then quickly entered to be greeted by

Turkish Baths in Jermyn Street, in *The Illustrated London News*, July 1862.

'a horrifying spectacle' – the old man prone on the floor, his fingers so badly scorched that 'they would have fallen with touching'.[16] A coroner's inquest found that he had toppled onto the flue and died from his burns.

These two deaths did nothing to check Urquhart's enthusiasm or to check his efforts to establish Turkish baths around the country. 'Turkish Baths are diffusing themselves like asteroids in November', declared a journalist in *The Reasoner* in 1861.[17] Indeed, there were ten Turkish baths in London by the end of 1861, including one in Upper Berkeley Square that catered to horses. In 1864 the Great Western Railway provided Turkish baths for railwaymen and their families in Swindon, and a year later inexpensive Turkish baths became available at the Ragged Castle and Workmen's Hall in Notting Hill. The most famous was the London Hammam, which opened at 76 Jermyn Street in London in 1862, operated by Urquhart's London & Provincial Turkish Bath Company. Patronized by the sons of Queen Victoria, it featured attendants who handed bathers five towels, one to go around the waist, another over the shoulders, and the other three for wiping and drying. The shampoo – a combination of massage and body wash – was performed by a bath-man wearing camel-hair gloves. Afterwards, in the cooling room, bathers were plied with coffee, fruit and sherbet as attendants waved feathered fans at them.

All of this Eastern-style exoticism was too much for some. In 1861 a distinguished scientist, Dr J.L.W. Thudichum, protested: 'Can the active, fox-hunting, cricketing, boating Englishman bear the same kind of treatment that benefits and gratifies the indolent, languid, luxurious Turk?'[18] Dr Thudichum was, ironically, a German. The answer to his question was, it seems, an enthusiastic affirmative: some 600 Turkish baths opened in Britain during the second half of the nineteenth century.

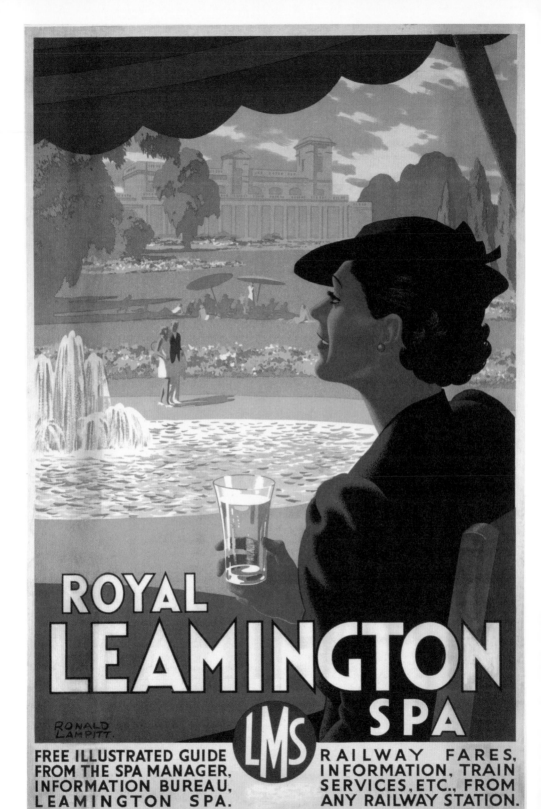

TEN

Leisure and Luxury

THE MODERN SPA

In 1917 Heaton Hall in Manchester was home to 4,000 wounded soldiers under the care of a Canadian physician, Major Robert Tait McKenzie. Before the war, Dr Tait McKenzie had been director of the Physical Education Department at the University of Pennsylvania. As a surgeon in the Royal Army Medical Corps, he became a specialist in treating and rehabilitating the wounded, who suffered from everything from dysentery and typhoid fever to trench foot, shell shock and shrapnel wounds. He concentrated on getting his patients to perform gymnastic manoeuvres and take the fresh air in Heaton Park.

Dr Tait McKenzie had one other method of improving the lives of his injured soldiers: he designed a hydrotherapy bath for them, which took twelve patients at a time, as well as a whirlpool bath. His establishment soon became known as the Pool of Bethesda because of the good results achieved among the patients. There was nothing miraculous or even exceptional about the waters, which merely came, like the rest of the city's water, from Manchester's reservoirs. But Tait McKenzie heated the waters as high as 80°C (176°F) and discovered that many of his patients derived clear

The London, Midland and Scottish Railway's alluring 1937 poster for Royal Leamington Spa.

benefits from this water cure. A Manchester newspaper reported: 'It is believed that this "whirl bath" has a special action due to the movement of the water, and the hydro-massage treatment which follows supplements its curative action.'[1]

The First World War created casualties on an unprecedented scale. Hydrotherapy offered a way of treating men who had been devastated by dreadful wounds, mental as well as physical. As the guns blazed on the Western Front, the Royal Society of Medicine established an inquiry investigating the merits of treating wounded soldiers with hydrotherapy. Their recommendation confirmed that spa treatments were particularly beneficial to soldiers suffering from shell shock, but also neurasthenia, stiff or wasted limbs, rapid heart rate and rheumatism. Once they were approved, the War Office advised committees to be created at established spas to work out suitable regimes for injured soldiers. By early 1917, 2,220 military personnel were treated at Bath; 3,500 at Harrogate; 17,102 at Droitwich Brine Baths; 276 at Woodhall Spa; and 307 at Llandrindod Wells in Wales. Between 1914 and 1916, 1,926 men were treated at the Devonshire Hospital in Buxton, at a specialized hospital wing built by Canadians for hydrological treatment for their soldiers.[2]

These treatment facilities were to mark the last great course of water cures in Britain. The medical establishment in the twentieth century would, by and large, turn away from hydrotherapy and steam baths, placing its faith in other therapies and treatments, especially pharmaceutical ones. The survival of spas into the twenty-first century would be a result of their ability to adapt to different needs of clients, particularly those in search of relaxing and luxurious recreations and treatments of a sort that the best spas had always offered.

Following the Great War, medical opinion was divided over the efficacy of spa treatments. In the early 1920s those medics in favour published *The Official Handbook of the British Spa Federation* as an aid to

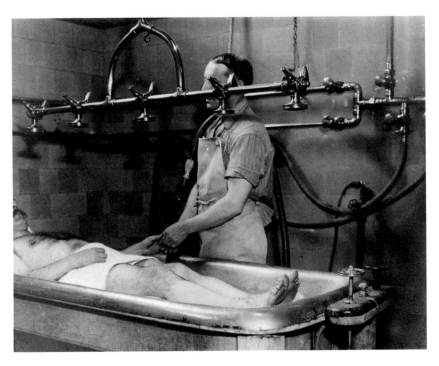

Treatment in the Aix-bath in Devonshire Hospital, Buxton, c.1940s.

the medical profession. 'The British spas are perhaps the most tonic in the world', the handbook declared, defining 'tonic' as the bracing qualities of the climate.[3] Patients were advised to take exercise in the open air and keep stimulating amusements at a minimum – very different from the expectations of early spa patrons. Bath, Chelten-ham, Droitwich and Leamington Spa were considered by supporters to be the most effective in treating nervous and mental fatigue. For patients suffering chronic toxaemia, requiring bowel movements, the waters of Cheltenham and Harrogate were recommended, whereas the spas of Leamington and Llandrindod Wells were visited by those in need of a diuretic.

The numbers of people visiting spas dwindled in the interwar years. Over the course of the decades that followed, many of the traditional English spas lost their function due to the combination of modern medicine – committed as it was to surgical procedures and pharmaceutical therapy rather than mineral waters and whirlpool baths – and the establishment of the National Health Service. In an effort to protect their interests, the combination of local authorities and private companies that owned spas established organizations such as the British Spa Federation (founded in 1916), the International Society of Medical Hydrology (1921) and the British Health Resorts Association (1932). Spas also undertook extensive advertising campaigns. In the early 1930s the six well-established spas of Bath, Buxton, Cheltenham, Droitwich, Harrogate and Tunbridge Wells joined forces in a national advertising campaign. Using the slogan 'Health Comes Happily at British Spas', they argued that spas promoted health by using 'the most modern hydrological methods known to science'.[4] Droitwich even advertised cocktail parties for bathers, with drinks served on floating tables.

The Second World War dramatically impacted health tourism, which was exacerbated by the requisitioning by the government of many spa buildings and hospitals. Cheltenham's Pittville Pump Room accommodated British and American troops, while the Ben Rhydding Hydro in Ilkley housed the government's Wool Control Board. The experience of Smedley's establishment in Matlock was typical. By the early twentieth century the spa was run more like a five-star hotel, the austere regime abandoned in favour of a magnificent dining hall with seating for 300 people, who were served by chefs trained in London. There was also a library, a billiard room, tennis courts, manicured gardens, and even a hairdresser installed in the basement. By 1939, the establishment boasted hundreds of different treatments and baths, a staff of 60 male and female bath specialists, and servants who could provide food at any hour of the night. During the Second World War, however, it was taken over by the government for a School of Military Intelligence (the future actor Dirk Bogarde was among the students, training

in the interpretation of aerial photography). In 1946 it reverted
to a hotel, but within a decade it languished. At one point in the
summer of 1954, when it offered 270 rooms, only 150 guest were
registered. Soon afterwards the shareholders accepted the offer of
Derbyshire County Council to take it over for their administrative
offices.[5]

Indeed, the post-war period was a grim one for spas as they were
overtaken by an enormous change in healthcare: the launching in
July 1948 of the National Health Service (NHS). Its aim was to
provide, at public expense, medical, dental and nursing care to
everyone in the country. The NHS was to have a further impact.
Most spas at this time were either in private ownership or in that
of the local authorities, but in each case they realized their survival
depended on providing medical services for the state. The spas in
Bath, Leamington Spa, Droitwich, Woodhall and Buxton were
quick to arrange contracts with their local NHS providers, receiving
patients for hydrotherapy treatments as part of their cure. But NHS
supervision of healthcare meant the three-week spa cure – the
duration recommended – was phased out due to cost, and most
NHS patients lucky enough to be sent to a spa were funded only for
daily outpatient visits. (A notable exception was patients at Stoke
Mandeville Hospital, where those with spinal injuries and paralysis
due to polio received treatment in a hydrotherapy pool opened in
the summer of 1953.) As everyone in Britain expected free medical
treatment, the entire private healthcare sector was hugely dimin-
ished, spa resorts and hydrotherapy included.

If the traditional spas declined in the post-war years, seaside
resorts such as Brighton, Scarborough and Blackpool continued
to flourish during the summer months. Their popularity was due
to paid holidays for workers, more than 40 per cent of whom,
according to a 1953 report, chose the seaside for their vacation. The
highest visitor numbers in the decade after the war were recorded

in 1948 and 1949, thanks to wartime savings, gratuities and the lack of consumer goods. However, the writing was already on the wall by the early 1950s, as what the report called a 'change in pattern of British holidays' took hold, with vacationers increasingly plumping for European holidays. Before the war, the Continental boat trains were filled 'by members of the middle class', but in the 1950s 'the artisan, the typist, the clerk, and the shop assistant are discovering France, Switzerland, Spain and Italy'.[6] The tide for Britain's seaside resorts was turning.

As the NHS developed alternative ways to cure the population, beautiful old spa buildings and ancient wells were demolished or boarded up. Others fell victim to a more random damage, as in Harrogate, where the well heads for Magnesia Well were capped and the wells buried following damage by vandals in 1973. The magnificent Ben Rhydding Hydro in Ilkley was knocked down in 1955; only the golf course survives today. All that remains of others – Leamington Spa's Aylesford Well, St Ann's Well in Brighton, and Bristol Hotwells – are memorial stones marking their positions. The Hay Well in Malvern, which once fed Dr Gully's Hay Well Baths and treated Charles Darwin, is now beneath the car park of the Baptist church erected in 1893. The spring waters of Scarborough are hidden beneath a utility hole in the Grand Pavilion. The Lower Assembly Rooms in Bath were demolished in 1933 for a new road system. Underground toilets erected on part of the site closed in the 1980s, only to be converted and reopened as a nightclub named the Island Club. Due to subsidence this too was forced to close. A plaque commemorates the spot, but it is colloquially known as 'Bog Island' after the public lavatories – the toilets evidently lingering longer in the public consciousness than the Assembly Rooms.

Nor have the original mineral baths fared well either. The thermal baths situated at the end of Buxton's Crescent closed in 1972; the site is now a row of shops. In Droitwich, the Royal Brine

The impressively domed Montpellier Well In Cheltenham (now the Ivy Brasserie).

Baths closed their doors in the 1930s, and St Andrew's Brine Baths in 1975. The New Victoria Baths in Low Harrogate were demolished in 1931, replaced by municipal offices. All mineral water outlets and baths in Bath Spa were turned off in 1978 after a young bather died after contracting an amoebic infection, *Naegleria fowleri*, from the mineral waters. From then on, the Royal Bath Mineral Hospital – which closed its doors in 2019 – used heated tap water.

Fortunately, many spa buildings are listed for their beauty and historical importance, thus preventing their demolition. No longer in use for their original purpose, many have been converted for other employment. The Magnesia Well Pump Room in Harrogate and Ilkley's White Wells both operate as cafés. A Chinese restaurant has leased the Grand Pump Room in Harrogate since 2008, and in 2017 the Montpellier Rotunda in Cheltenham was sold to the Ivy restaurant chain. The Pittville Pump Room in Cheltenham is a successful wedding venue, Smedley's Hydro in Matlock continues as the administrative headquarters for Derbyshire County Council, and the Royal Pump Rooms in Leamington Spa now host the Leamington Spa Art Gallery & Museum as well as a library, a visitor information centre and the Royal Spa Centre's Box Office. Gulliver's Kingdom, a theme park, operates on the site of the Royal Hotel in Matlock. Dr Gully's Holyrood House for women in Malvern is presently the surgery for an acupuncturist and herbalist.

The most common reuse of spa buildings in the twenty-first century is for private accommodation. Wells House, Rock House, Dr Gully's Tudor House and Dr Wilson's Priessnitz Hydro – all in Malvern – have been converted into private apartments. The Upper Assembly Rooms in Leamington Spa were converted into Woodward's department store in 1908, but in 2005 the premises was redeveloped into individual shops with private apartments above. Margate's Royal Sea Bathing Hospital, with direct access to the beach, has also been refurbished and turned into private apartments. There are even several luxury beach houses built on the site, and planning applications have been put forward to convert the hospital mortuary and chapel into private dwellings. Meanwhile the shelter in which T.S. Eliot wrote part of *The Waste Land* survives, listed by English Heritage in 2009.

AURA WRAPS AND FIRE FACIALS

The majority of England's spas are hardly the establishments they once were in the days when taking the waters was an annual ritual conducted for both health and entertainment. However, many spa towns still attract tourists, situated as they so often are in urban areas with elegant architecture and beautiful, accessible locations. History, tourism and the wellness industry have come together, offering commercial incentives to refurbish some of the old sites, as in Buxton, where a £50 million project has recently witnessed the renovation of the Crescent as a 5-star hotel with eighty bedrooms

A bathing machine containing a sauna commissioned by local firm Haeckels, on the beach at Margate, 2019.

and a thermal natural mineral spa. Bath, the template for so many other spa towns, continues to thrive, with its Roman Baths – the subject of a fifteen-year redevelopment – attracting a million visitors a year.[7] An even bigger project for the city was the renovation of five listed buildings in Bath by the Thermal Development Company (TDC) and partners. It is now possible to follow the example of so many eighteenth-century visitors and bathe once again in the Cross Bath and the Hot Bath. The renovated Pump Room, with Beau Nash's statue still on show, houses a restaurant, and visitors can sample the waters – which, for the peace of mind of any latter-day Matthew Brambles, have been treated – at the restored pump. But the crowning achievement was the opening of the New Royal Bath, which has two natural thermal baths, an open-top rooftop pool, and an indoor pool with a jet stream that gently pushes swimmers around the pool. There is a Wellness Suite that includes two aromatic steam rooms, an ice chamber, an infrared sauna, a relaxation room, a café, and no fewer than twenty-seven spa treatment rooms.

As the example of the New Royal Bath indicates, everything old is new again. Spas and public baths have not disappeared, of course. Having reinvented themselves, they function as an important part of the wellness industry, albeit associated with leisure, beauty and

The rooftop pool at the Thermae Bath Spa in Bath.

well-being rather than convalescence and disease. The focus of a modern spa experience is on beauty treatments, weight loss and sometimes meditation – along with a panoply of activities such as t'ai chi, power walks and Gymstick exercises.

In 1851 the English journalist Joseph Leech spent three weeks in wet sheets. A modern-day Leech might expect to spend an hour or two encountering even odder treatments. Today's spa treatments include anti-cellulite massages, lympathic drainage facials, aura wraps, virtual reality headsets, snake massages (exactly what it says on the tin) and baths in anything from seaweed to coffee, milk or beer. It has not yet arrived in the UK, but in China the brave or the desperate can get an anti-ageing 'fire facial' in which an alcohol-soaked cloth is placed on the face and then set alight before, a second or two later, the therapist extinguishes it.

If earlier spas featured bath-men and hydrotherapy experts, the staff of modern spas therefore require a cast of fitness instructors, massage therapists, nutritionists, aromatherapists, pedicure technicians and various sorts of beautician. Exfoliation is a popular treatment, with 'ice fountains' that stimulate the circulation and rejuvenate the skin. Likewise depilation, with wax used to remove body hair from the face or private parts. This procedure offers choices that include bikini waxes, Brazilians, manzilians and snail trail waxes (removing the hair along the 'happy trail' running south from the belly button). Or clients can enjoy Watsu massages: a therapy in which practitioners support them in warm, chest-deep water, cradling and floating them in a kind of slow aquatic dance.

Contemporary spas include 'sensory showers' that, at the touch of a button, can replicate everything from a gentle mist to the splattering drops of a tropical thunderstorm. Lighting and sound effects, including mood music, gentle percussion and tweeting birds, complete the holistic showering experience. Aromatherapy showers mix essential oils with the water to stimulate the senses. Other spas feature purpose-built snow cabins, chilled to freezing temperatures in order to boost metabolism. Some luxury spas even offer an hour in a 'salt cave' that aims to improve breathing and circulation, while others feature personal relaxation pods and flotation tanks. Precious stones and metals such as gold, silver and diamonds are applied in face masks, creams, wraps and massages, and even whiskies and liqueurs are pressed into service, mixed with a golden mud and applied to the body.

One hotel in London clears pores with a powder made from black diamonds. Michael La Beaume, obsessed as he was with 'checked perspiration', would be pleased, as he would be with the fact that some spas use electricity, offering galvanic baths and electrotherapy detoxes. Likewise, many British spas feature plunge pools, saunas and hammams: precisely the kinds of therapy that, a century and a half earlier, David Urquhart worked so hard to promote throughout the country. But no matter how exotic or even outlandish the techniques of modern spas, all of their treatments are part of a great British tradition of taking the waters.

Explanation of Spa Water

Please note that this book is not intended to provide medical or other health advice for readers, and these waters are not recommended for use without expert advice.

CHALYBEATE WATER Natural mineral springs containing iron salts: iron carbonate, manganese carbonate, calcium sulphate, magnesium sulphate, magnesium chloride, sodium chloride and potassium chloride. The dissolved iron in the water leaves an unappetizing brown scum floating on the surface. Notable chalybeate springs are in Cheltenham, Harrogate, Tunbridge Wells, Hove (Brighton) and Scarborough. In Trefriw Spa, North Wales, the iron concentration is more than 500 mg/litre, and the water is marketed as 'liquid iron' or Spatone. It was once prescribed as a tonic for iron deficiency, anaemia and even tuberculosis.

SULPHUR WATER Water containing hydrogen sulphide or metallic sulfides. The bacteria in the sulphur create the smell of rotten eggs usually associated with sulphur waters. Some compounds in sulphur are antiseptic and shown to be useful for a number of skin complaints. If the waters are hot, they can have a stimulating effect on the skin. Drinking sulphur water can cause stomach upsets and diarrhoea.

SALINE WATER Saline water contains a high concentration of dissolved salts: sodium chloride, sodium sulphate and magnesium sulphate.

Harrogate Royal Baths, c.1900.

The salts are not absorbed into the bloodstream, causing a purgative effect, and by osmosis draw fluid from the surrounding tissues. It was commonly thought that the removal of fluid from the body lowered blood pressure and was therefore beneficial for inflammatory and congestive diseases such as dropsy. It was also recommended for gout and liver complaints.

BRINE There is a greater concentration of salt in brine than in saline water or seawater. It occurs naturally in salt lakes (the Dead Sea in Israel, Jordan and the West Bank), in the earth's crust (Droitwich), and within brine pools on the ocean floor.

SEAWATER Water from the ocean or a sea. There are roughly 35 grams (1.2 oz) of dissolved salts for every litre of seawater. Seawater consists of oxygen, hydrogen, chlorine, sodium, magnesium, sulphur, calcium, potassium, bromine, carbon and vanadium. It is dangerous for humans to consume too much.

Notes

ONE

1. www.director.co.uk/7891-uk-spa-industry-booming (accessed 10 October 2019); www.statista.com/statistics/200141/us-spa-industry-location-numbers (accessed 10 October 2019).
2. Richard Russell, *A Dissertation on the Use of Sea Water in the Diseases of the Glands*, W. Owen, London, 1860, pp. 230, 264, 290, 256.
3. Norman Hammond and David Sanderson, 'Brits Beat Romans to the Baths', *The Times*, 11 September 2019, p. 11.
4. Seneca, *Epistles*, vol. 1, trans. Richard M. Gummere, Loeb Classical Library 75, Heinemann, London, 1917, Epistle 61, p. 373.
5. Ibid., p. 374.
6. See Cynthia Imogen Hammond, *Architects, Angels, Activists and the City of Bath, 1765–1965: Engaging with Women's Spatial Interventions in Buildings and Landscape*, Ashgate, Farnham, 2012, p. 34.
7. Jules Michelet, *La Sorcière*, E. Dentu, Paris, 1862, p. 110.
8. Quoted in Ian D. Rotherham, *Spas and Spa Visiting*, Shire, Oxford, 2014, p. 1.
9. Quoted in Gerrit Bos, 'Maimonides on the Preservation of Health', *Journal of the Royal Asiatic Society*, vol. 4, no. 2, July 1994, p. 231.
10. Quoted in Katherine Ashenburg, *The Dirt on Clean: An Unsanitized History*, Vintage Canada, Toronto, 2008, p. 100.
11. *The Free Press*, vol. 6, London, 1858, p. 129.
12. Quoted in Michael W. Greenslade, *Catholic Staffordshire, 1500–1850,* Gracewing, Leominster, 2006, p. 21.
13. The Wake refers to observance of local saints' days. Church services commenced at sunset on the Saturday and the night prayer was a vigil. This was followed by public entertainment, funfairs, games and trips to the seaside.
14. Quoted in John Guy, *Queen of Scots: The True Life of Mary Stuart,* Houghton Mifflin, Boston MA, 2004, p. 435.
15. Originally in Latin, *Buxtona quae calidae celebrabere nomine lympea, Forte mihi posthac non adeunda, vale*. William Camden, *Survey of the County of Derbyshire*, 1610; quoted in Mike Langham, 'Things written in the glasse windowes at Buxstons', *Derbyshire Miscellany: The Local History Bulletin of the Derbyshire Archaeological Society* 15, pt 1, Spring 1998, pp. 9–21.

16. James P. Carley, 'Henry Parker', *Oxford Dictionary of National Biography*, Oxford University Press, Oxford, 2004–16.

17. Eamon Duffy, 'William Allen', *Oxford Dictionary of National Biography,* Oxford University Press, Oxford, 2004–16.

TWO

1. William Shakespeare, *The Oxford Shakespeare: The Complete Works*, 2nd edn, Oxford University Press, Oxford, 2005, p. 798.

2. Ibid.

3. Quoted in Randle Wilbraham Falconer, *The Baths and Mineral Waters of Bath*, Royal College of Physicians of London, London, 1867, pp. xiv–xv.

4. *Calendar of State Papers: Of the Reigns of Edward VI, Mary, Elizabeth and James I. 1547–[1625] Preserved in the State Paper Department of Her Majesty's Public Record Office,* Domestic series, vol. 10, p. 391.

5. Phyllis Hembry, *The English Spa 1560–1815: A Social History*, Athlone, London, 1990, p. 41.

6. *Calendar of State Papers, Domestic Series, of the Reign of James I: 1611–1618*, ed. Mary Anne Everett Green, Longman, London, 1858, pp. 285, 300.

7. Hembry, *The English Spa 1560–1815*, p. 42.

8. Ibid., p. 43.

9. Victor Slater, 'Dudley North, third Baron North', *Oxford Dictionary of National Biography*, Oxford University Press, Oxford, 2004.

10. Hembry, *The English Spa 1560–1815*, pp. 46, 49.

11. Henry Pownall, *Some Particulars Relating to the History of Epsom*, J. Hearne, London, 1825, pp. 57–8.

12. *The Gentleman's Magazine* 35, 1851, London, p. 253.

13. Edmund Deane, *Spadacrene Anglica; or the English Spaw-Fountain*, London, 1626, ch. 9, p. 14.

14. Hembry, *The English Spa 1560–1815*, p. 51.

15. Ibid., p. 52.

16. John French, *The Yorkshire Spaw, or, a treatise of four famous medical wells, viz. the spas, or Vitrioline Well; the Stinking or Sulphur Well; the Dropping or Petrifying Well, and St. Mungo's Well near Knaresburgh in Yorkshire*, London, 1651.

17. Quoted in William Grainge, *The History and Topography of Harrogate, and the Forest of Knaresborough*, John Russell Smith, London, 1871, p. 113.

18. Hembry, *The English Spa 1560–1815*, p. 62.

19. Ibid., p. 73.

20. Quoted in James Joseph Sheahan and T. Whellan, *History and Topography of the City of York; and the North Riding of Yorkshire; Embracing a General Review of the Early History of Great Britain, and a General History and Description of the County of York*, vol. 1., T. Whellan, Beverley, 1857, p. 718.

21. Ibid.

22. From Sadler's Wells website, www.sadlerswells.com.

23. Samuel Pepys, *The Diary of Samuel Pepys M.A. F.R.S.: 1664*, Outlook Verlag, Frankfurt, 2018, p. 125.

24. Daniel Defoe, *A Tour thro' the Whole Island of Great Britain* [1724–27], vol. 1, London, 1724, pp. 107–8.

25. Walter Thornbury, 'Coldbath Fields and Spa Fields', in *Old and New London*, vol. 2, Cassell, Petter & Galpin, London, 1878, pp. 298–306.

THREE

1. John Wood, *A Description of Bath*, London, 1765, pp. 216–17.
2. The branding of vagabonds was abolished by the Poor Law Act of 1601 (43 Eliz.I.c2), only to be replaced by the dispatching of beggars to Houses of Correction – the precursor of the Victorian workhouse – that ensured that the fit but jobless could be set to work.
3. Andrew Winter, 'Bath', *The Land We Live in, a Pictorial and Literary Sketch-book of the British Empire*, vol. 3, Charles Knight, London, 1847–50, p. 28.
4. Dudley Ryder, *The Diary of Dudley Ryder 1715–1716*, ed. William Matthews, Methuen, London, 1939, p. 240.
5. Gil Blas is the protagonist in Alain-Rene Lesage's novel *Histoire de Gil Blas de Santillana* (1715–35), who is lowly born but through a series of adventures becomes the king's favourite at court.
6. Oliver Goldsmith, *The Life of Beau Nash*, 2nd edn, London, 1762, p. 8.
7. Captain Thomas Webster had taken up residence in Bath and unofficially took over organizing entertainments from the Duke of Beaufort, who held private dances at his estate in Badminton, 14 miles from Bath. Webster took it upon himself to organize balls at the town hall for about ten couples by invitation only.
8. It was demolished in 1738 and replaced by the Mineral Water Hospital.
9. Edward Ward, *A Step to the Bath with a Character of the Place*, London, 1700, p. 12.
10. A large ballroom was added to Harrison's Assembly Rooms in 1720, and nearly thirty years later the rooms were enlarged further. By 1810 these rooms became known as the Kingston Assembly rooms, which were destroyed by fire in 1820. They were rebuilt but ultimately demolished for road improvements in 1933.
11. *An Essay Against Too Much Reading*, London, 1728, pp. 20–22.
12. Goldsmith, *The Life of Beau Nash*, Preface.
13. 'Bath Rules laid down by Richard Nash, Esq., M.C. Put up by Authority in the Pump Room, and observed at Bath Assemblies during his reign', 1707; quoted in Goldsmith, *The Life of Beau Nash*, pp. 20–21.
14. Eliza Haywood, *Bath Intrigues: In Four Letters to a Friend in London*, 3rd edn, J. Roberts, London, 1725, p. 16.
15. Richard Brinsley Sheridan, *The Rivals: A Comedy. As it is Acted at the Theatre-Royal in Covent-Garden*, 5.2.1–2, London, 1775.
16. Goldsmith, *The Life of Beau Nash*, pp. 5, 22.
17. Quoted in ibid., pp. 22–3.
18. Ryder, *The Diary of Dudley Ryder 1715–1716*, p. 240.
19. Robert Whatley, *Characters at the Hot-Well, Bristol, in September, and at Bath, in October, 1723*, James Lacy, London, 1723, pp. vi–vii.
20. When the Bath Pump Room was enlarged in 1751 the Bath Corporation commissioned a bust of Nash, which stands proudly in the present Pump Room.
21. J. Sprange, *The Tunbridge Wells Guide, or an Account of the Ancient and Present State of that Place, to which is Added a Particular Description of the Towns and Villages, ... within the Circumference of Sixteen Miles*, J. Sprange, Tunbridge Wells, 1780.
22. Ibid., p. 288.
23. Goldsmith, *The Life of Beau Nash*, p. 19.
24. Quoted in Philip Carter, 'Richard (Beau) Nash', *Oxford Dictionary of National Biography*.
25. Goldsmith, *The Life of Beau Nash*, p. 61.
26. *The Bath Contest: Being a Collection of all the Papers, Advertisements, &c. Published Before and Since The Death of Mr. Derrick, By the Candidates For the Office of Master of Ceremonies, And their Friends, Digested in Regular Order*, Bath, 1769, pp. 44–6.
27. *The Bath and Bristol Chronicle*, 13 April 1769.

28. Thomas Short, *An Essay towards a Natural, Experimental, and Medicinal History of the principle Mineral Waters of Cumberland, Northumberland, Westmoreland ... : to which is added, a short discourse on cold and tepid bathing, and a table of the temperature ... ; being the second volume of The mineral waters of England*, Sheffield, 1740.

FOUR

1. Thomas Guidott, *The Register of Bath*, London, 1694, p. 149.
2. Quoted in Daniel Cottom, 'In the Bowels of the Novel: The Exchange of Fluids in the Beau Monde', *Novel: A Forum on Fiction* 32, Spring 1999, p. 160.
3. William Falconer, *An Essay on Bath Waters*, London, 1772, p. 1.
4. John Speed, 'A Commentary on Sea Water', in Richard Russell, *A Dissertation on the Use of Sea Water*, London, 1750, pp. 151–3.
5. John Macky, *A Journey Through England*, London, 1722, pp. 129–30.
6. Celia Fiennes, *The Illustrated Journeys of Celia Fiennes 1685–c.1712*, ed. Christopher Morris, Short Run Press, Exeter, 2002, p. 46.
7. Alex Sutherland, M.D., *Attempts to Retrieve Ancient Medical Doctrines*, London, 1763, p. 6.
8. Samuel Gale, 'A Tour Through Several Parts of England 1705', quoted in John Nichols, *Antiquities in Lincolnshire: being the third volume of the Bibliotheca Topographica Britannica*, vol. 3, London, 1790, p. 7.
9. Fiennes, *The Illustrated Journeys of Celia Fiennes 1685–c1712*, p. 45.
10. Tobias Smollett, *The Expedition of Humphry Clinker* (1771), ed. Peter Miles, Everyman, London, 1993, p. 45, Winifred Jenkins to Mrs Mary Jones, at Brambleton-Hall, Bath, 26 April.
11. Fiennes, *The Illustrated Journeys of Celia Fiennes 1685–c.1712*, p. 44.
12. Quoted in Phyllis Hembry, *The English Spa 1560–1815: A Social History*, Athlone Press, London, 1990, p. 57.
13. William Schellinks, *The Journal of William Schellinks' Travels in England 1661–1663*, trans. and ed. M. Exwood and H.L. Lehman, Camden 5th ser., vol. 1, Royal Historical Society, London, 1993, p. 106.
14. Samuel Gale, *A Tour Through Several Parts of England 1705*, quoted in John Nichols, *Antiquities in Lincolnshire: being the third volume of* the Bibliotheca Topographica Britannica, London, 1790, p. 22.
15. Schellinks, *The Journal of William Schellinks' Travels in England 1661–1663*, p. 106.
16. Samuel Pepys, *Memoirs of Samuel Pepys, Esq., F.R.S., Secretary to the Admiralty comprising his diary from 1659 to 1669*, ed. Richard Lord Braybrooke, 2nd edn, vol. IV, Henry Colburn, London, 1828, p. 127.
17. Quoted in A. Barbeau, *Life and Letters at Bath in the XVIIIth Century*, with a preface by Austin Dobson, William Heinemann, London, 1904, p. 8 n4.
18. Tobias Smollett, *An Essay on the External Use of Water*, London, 1752, p. 34.
19. Tobias Smollett, *The Expedition of Humphrey Clinker* (1771), ed. Peter Miles, Everyman, London, 1993, p. 47.
20. James Roberts, *The Diseases of Bath: A Satire unadorn'd with a Frontispiece*, London, 1737, pp. 3–15.
21. Christopher Anstey, *The New Bath Guide: or, Memoirs of the B–R–D Family in a series of Poetical Epistles*, London, 1766, pp. 36–42.
22. Smollett, *The Expedition of Humphrey Clinker*, p. 47.
23. Pierce Egan, *Walks through Bath*, Bath, 1819, p. 91n.
24. Macky, *A Journey Through England*, vol. 2, p. 130.
25. Anstey, *The New Bath Guide: or, Memoirs of the B–R–D Family*, p. 38.
26. Fiennes, *The Illustrated Journeys of Celia Fiennes 1685–c.1712*, p. 46.
27. Smollett, *An Essay on the External Use of Waters*, p. 22.

28. Bagnio in this context means bathhouse and not a brothel.
29. Anstey, *The New Bath Guide: or, Memoirs of the B—R—D Family*, p. 36.
30. Daniel Defoe, *A Tour thro' the Whole Island of Great Britain* [1724—27], vol. 2, London, 1725, p. 51.
31. Quoted in Briony Hudson, 'Gout: A History of Theories and Treatments', *The Pharmaceutical Journal*, December 2009.
32. N.A. Shadick et al., 'Effect of Low Level Lead Exposure on Hyperuricemia and Gout among Middle Aged and Elderly Men: The Normative Aging Study', *Journal of Rheumatology* 27, July 2000, pp. 1708—12.
33. William Buchan, *Domestic Medicine, or a Treatise on the Prevention and cure of Diseases by Regimen and Simple Medicines*, J. Smith, London, 1830, p. 239.
34. Quoted in Hudson, 'Gout: A History of Theories and Treatments'.
35. Robert Pierce, *The History and Memoirs of the Bath: containing Observations on what Cures have been there wrought, both by Bathing and Drinking those Waters*, London, 1713, p. 17.
36. Ibid., pp. 14, 169—70.
37. John Wynter, *Of Bathing in the Hot-Baths at Bathe*, London, 1728, p. 53.
38. Audrey Heywood, 'A Trial of the Bath Waters: The Treatment of Lead Poisoning', *Medical History*, Supplement 10, 1990, pp. 82—101. See also Audrey Heywood et al., 'Effect of Immersion on Urinary Lead Excretion', *British Journal of Industrial Medicine* 43, 1986, pp. 713—15.
39. See José Manuel Carbajo and Francisco Maraver, 'Sulphurous Mineral Waters: New Applications for Health', in *Evidence-Based Complementary and Alternative Medicine*, eCAM vol. 2017 (2017): 8034084. doi:10.1155/2017/8034084 (accessed 14 October 2019).
40. Defoe, *A Tour thro' the Whole Island of Great Britain*, vol. 2, p. 52.
41. David Kinneir, *A New Essay on the Nerves, and the Doctrine of Animal Spirits Rationally Considered*, London, 1739, p. 70.
42. Fanny Burney, *Evelina, or the History of a Young Lady's Introduction to the World*, Paris, 1838, pp. 324—5.
43. John Feltham, *A Guide to All the Watering and Sea-Bathing Places*, R. Phillips, London, 1803, p. 27.
44. Buchan, *Domestic Medicine, or a Treatise on the Prevention and cure of Diseases by Regimen and Simple Medicines*, p. 401.
45. Charles Perry, *An Enquiry into the Nature and Principles of the Spaw Waters*, London, 1734, p. 5.
46. Smollett, *The Expedition of Humphrey Clinker*, pp. 166—7.
47. Richard Russell, *A Dissertation on the Use of Sea Water in the Diseases of the Glands*, London, 1760, p. 230.
48. Buchan, *Domestic Medicine, or a Treatise on the Prevention and cure of Diseases by Regimen and Simple Medicines*, p. 404.
49. Ibid., p. 399.
50. Ibid., p. 402.
51. Anon, *Tunbrigalia: or, Tunbridge Miscellanies, For the Year 1719*, pt 1, 2nd edn, London, 1719, pp. 46—7.
52. For examples of the 'bowels of the earth' trope, see Cottom, 'In the Bowels of the Novel', pp. 157—86.
53. *Elizabeth Montagu, the Queen of the Bluestockings*, vol. 2, ed. Emily J. Climenson, Cambridge University Press, Cambridge, 2011, p. 31.
54. Anstey, *The New Bath Guide: or, Memoirs of the B—R—D Family*, p. 6.
55. 'A Letter from Tunbridge to a Friend in London; being a Character of the Wells,

and Company there', *The Tunbridge and Bath Miscellany for the Year 1714. Giving an exact description of those places, with characters of the Company*, London, 1714, n.pag.

56. John Leake, *A Practical Essay on Diseases of the Viscera*, London, 1792, p. 327.

57. T. Short, *The Contents, Virtues, and Uses of Nevil-Holt Spaw-Water*, London, 1749, pp. 54–5.

58. Quoted in 'When the Duchess Paid a Visit', *Scarborough News*, 15 July 2011; www.pressreader.com/uk/the-scarborough-news/20110715/282033323848441 (accessed 3 March 2020).

59. J.P. de Limbourg, *New Amusements of the German Spa*, vol. 2, London, 1764, pp. 71–2.

60. Defoe, *A Tour thro' the Whole Island of Great Britain*, vol. 3, p. 57.

61. Sylvia McIntyre, 'The Mineral Water Trade in the Eighteenth Century', *Journal of Transport History* 2, 1973, p. 8.

62. Buchan, *Domestic Medicine, or a Treatise on the Prevention and cure of Diseases by Regimen and Simple Medicines*, p. 408.

63. Robert Whytt, 'Of the Various Strengths of Different Lime-Waters', *Essays and Observations, Physical and Literary*, Edinburgh, 1754, p. 375.

64. *The Works of George Berkeley, Bishop of Cloyne*, vol. 5, ed. A.A. Luce and T.E. Jessop, Thomas Nelson, Edinburgh, 1948–57, p. 175.

65. W.S. Lewis, ed., *Horace Walpole's Correspondence with Sir Horace Mann*, vol. 2, Yale University Press, New Haven CT, 1955, p. 451.

66. James Jurin, *A Letter to the Right Reverend the Bishop of Cloyne, Occasion'd by His Lordship's Treatise on the Virtues of Tar-Water*, London, 1744, p. 39. For a good study of Berkeley's tar-water, see Scott Breuninger, 'A Panacea for the Nation: Berkeley's Tar-water and Irish Domestic Development', *Études Irlandaises* 34, 2009, pp. 29–41.

67. Thomas Sydenham, cited in Helen King, 'Green Sickness: Hippocrates, Galen and the Origins of the "Disease of Virgins"', *International Journal of the Classical Tradition* 2, Winter 1996, p. 373.

68. Quoted in Helen King, *The Disease of Virgins: Green Sickness, Chlorosis and the Problems of Puberty*, Routledge, London, 2004, p. 113.

69. John C. Gunn, *Gunn's Domestic Medicine: Or Poor Man's Friend*, John M. Gallagher, Springfield OH, 1835, p. 398.

70. Quoted in King, 'Green Sickness', p. 379.

71. 'A Letter from Tunbridge to a Friend in London', n.pag.

72. Buchan, *Domestic Medicine, or a Treatise on the Prevention and cure of Diseases by Regimen and Simple Medicines*, p. 409.

73. 'An Account of Two Books', *Philosophical Transactions, Giving Some Accompt of the Present Undertakings, Studies, and Labours of the Ingenious in Many Considerable Parts of the World*, London, 1670, p. 1039.

FIVE

1. Tobias Smollett, *The Expedition of Humphrey Clinker* (1771), ed. Peter Miles, Everyman, London, 1993, p. 44.

2. *The Correspondence of Alexander Pope*, vol. 1, ed. George Sherburn, Clarendon Press, Oxford, 1956, p. 260, 6 October 1714.

3. Quoted in Ian C. Bradley, *Water Music: Music Making in the Spas of Europe and North America*, Oxford University Press, Oxford, 2010, p. 32.

4. Daniel Defoe, *A Tour thro' the Whole Island of Great Britain* [1724–27], vol. 2, London, 1725, p. 51.

5. Ibid., p. 55.

6. 'Bath Intrigues', in *The Works of the Earls of Rochester, Roscomon, and Dorset*, London, 1735, p. 66.

7. Smollett, *The Expedition of Humphrey Clinker*, p. 57.

8. Abbé Prévost, *Pour et Contre* 38, 1734, pp. 173–4.

9. *Mrs Montagu. 'Queen of the Blues': Her Letters and Friendships from 1762 to 1800*, ed. Reginald Bound, 2 vols, Constable, London, 1923, pp. 82, 81.

10. *Bath Chronicle*, 8 February 1776.

11. Jane Austen, *Northanger Abbey*, ed. Barbara M. Benedict and Deirdre Le Faye, Cambridge University Press, Cambridge, 2006, p. 21.

12. Quoted in Eliza Meteyard, *The Life of Josiah Wedgwood*, Hurst & Blackett, London, 1866, p. 254.

13. Quoted in Trevor Fawcett, 'Eighteenth-century Shops and the Luxury Trade', *Bath History* 3, 1990, p. 67.

14. The first craftsmen to make Tunbridge Ware famous were from the families Wise and Burrows. By the end of the nineteenth century many more people had learnt the trade, and techniques became even more intricate and skilled.

15. Blue John, also known as Derbyshire Spa, is extremely rare and has been over-mined. There are only two working Blue John mines left in the world, and one is in Treak Cliff Cavern in Castleton, Derbyshire. Treak Cliff Cavern mines only half a ton a year, exclusively for the purpose of having it made into jewellery.

16. 'An ice-cream parlour on Pultney Bridge', *Bath Chronicle*, 6 January 1774.

17. Bath City Library, MS B920 Edmund Rack, *A Disultory Journal of Events... at Bath*, entry for 22 January 1780.

18. *Bath Chronicle*, 19 December 1799.

19. Simeon Moreau, *A Tour to Cheltenham Spa; or, Gloucestershire display'd*, London, 1788, p. 33.

20. *A New and Enlarged Catalogue of Marshall's Circulating Library, top of Miso-Street, Bath*, Bath, 1794.

21. Mary Chandler, *A Description of Bath. A Poem. Humbly Inscribed to Her Royal Highness The Princess Amelia, With Several Other Poems*, London, 1734, p. 15.

22. Thomas Goulding, *An Essay Against Too Much Reading, with The Whole Lives and Proceeding of Sancho and Peepo, at Aix la Chapelle in Germany*, London, 1728, pp. 21–3.

23. Phillip Thicknesse, *New Prose Guide for the year 1778*, Bath, 1778, p. 38.

24. Smollett, *The Expedition of Humphrey Clinker*, p. 67.

25. Ibid., p. 68.

26. John Essex, *The Dancing Master: or, The Art of Dancing Explained. Done from the French of Monsieur Rameau by J. Essex, Dancing Master*, London, 1728, pp. 23, 34, 33.

27. Quoted in Bradley, *Water Music*, p. 41.

28. Samuel Pepys, Saturday 13 June 1668, in *Memoirs of Samuel Pepys, Esq., F.R.S., Secretary to the Admiralty comprising his diary from 1659 to 1669*, ed. Richard Lord Braybrooke, 2nd edn, vol. 4, Henry Colburn, London, 1828, p. 127.

29. Quoted in Bradley, *Water Music*, pp. 35–6.

30. Moreau, *A Tour to Cheltenham Spa*, p. 33.

31. *The Guardian* 174, 30 September 1713, p. 100.

32. *The Discoveries of John Poulter, alias Baxter; who was apprehended for robbing Dr. Ancock, of Salisbury*, 2nd edn, Sherbourne, 1753. In this edition there is no dedication to Nash.

33. Quoted in Michael Levey, *Sir Thomas Lawrence*, Yale University Press, New Haven CT and London, 2005, p. 46.

34. *Middlesex Journal*, 30 December 1775.

35. Quoted in 'Sarah Siddons', in Philip H. Highfill, Jr. et al., eds, *A Biographical Dictionary of Actors, Actresses, Musicians, Dancers, Managers, & Other Stage Personnel in London, 1660–1800*, vol. 14, Carbondale and Edwardsville, Southern Illinois University Press, 1991, p. 6.

SIX

1. Daniel Defoe, *The Fortunes and Misfortunes of the Famous Moll Flanders*, ed. G.A. Starr, Oxford University Press, Oxford, 1998, p. 106.
2. Oliver Goldsmith, *The Life of Beau Nash*, 2nd edn, London, 1762, Preface.
3. 'Sketches from the Portfolio of a Sexagenarian', *The New Monthly Magazine* (London), 1829, p. 195.
4. Karl Elze, *Lord Byron: A Biography*, J. Murray, London, 1872, p. 10.
5. Thomas Baker, *Tunbridge-Walks: or, the Yeoman of Kent*, Dublin, 1758, p. 47
6. Defoe, *The Fortunes and Misfortunes of the Famous Moll Flanders*, p. 106.
7. *The Bath, Bristol, Tunbridge and Epsom Miscellany*, London, 1735, pp. 21–2.
8. A. Barbeau, *Life and Letters at Bath in the XVIIIth Century*, with a preface by Austin Dobson, William Heinemann, London, 1904, p. 38.
9. *London Magazine,* December 1737, p. 685.
10. Quoted in Barbeau, *Life and Letters at Bath*, p. 96.
11. Ibid., p. 19 n1.
12. *The Scarborough Miscellany. An Original Collection of Poems, Odes, Tales, songs, Epigrams, etc. None which ever appear'd in Print before. By Several Hands*, London, 1732, p. 13.
13. Quoted in Barbeau, *Life and Letters at Bath*, p. 98.
14. *The Gentleman's Magazine* (London), 1731, pp. 396–7.
15. Quoted in Barbeau, *Life and Letters at Bath*, p. 99 n1.
16. *The Gentleman's Magazine* 66, 1789, pp. 1053–4.
17. Thomas Longueville, *Pryings among Private Papers*, Longman, Green, London, 1905, p. 154.
18. See Barbeau, *Life and Letters at Bath*, p. 30.
19. Richard Graves, *Euphrosyne, or, Amusements on the Road of Life in Verse*, London, 1783, pp. 84–5.
20. John Watkins, *Memoir of the Public and Private Life of the Right Honorable R.B. Sheridan*, vol. 1, London, 1817, p. 185.
21. Quoted in Barbeau, *Life and Letters at Bath*, p. 150 n3.
22. William Shakespeare, *The Oxford Shakespeare: The Complete Works*, 2nd edn, Oxford University Press, Oxford, 2005, p. 541.
23. Edward Ward, 'A Step to Bath', in *The Reformer*, 3rd edn, London, 1708, p. 158.
24. Daniel, Defoe, *A Tour thro' the Whole Island of Great Britain* [1724–27], vol. 2, London, 1725, p. 52.
25. Thomas D'Urfey, *The Bath: Or, The Western Lass*, London, 1701, p. 1.
26. Quoted in Trevor Fawcett, ed., *Voices of Eighteenth-Century Bath*, Ruton, Bath, 1995, p. 90.
27. Quoted in Tobias Smollett, *An Essay on the External Use of Water*, London, 1752, p. 48.
28. See Simon Varey, *Space and the Eighteenth-Century English Novel*, Cambridge University Press, Cambridge, 1990, p. 76.
29. Smollett, *An Essay on the External Use of Water*, p. 44.
30. Thomas Baker, *Tunbridge-Walks, or, the Yeoman of Kent; a Comedy*, Dublin, 1758, p. 8.
31. Ibid., p. 37.
32. Richard Ames, *An Old Poem on the mineral wells at Islington, near London, describing the company who resorted to them*, ed. J.O. Halliwell, esq., F.R.S., London, 1861. Reprinted from the poem entitled *Islington Wells, or the Threepenny-Academy* by Richard Ames, London, 1691.
33. Quoted in Barbeau, *Life and Letters at Bath*, p. 80.
34. 'A Letter from Tunbridge to a Friend in London; being a Character of the Wells, and Company there', *The Tunbridge and Bath Miscellany for the Year 1714 giving an exact description of those places, with characters of the Company*, London, 1714, n.pag.

35. 'Scarborough Wells: A Satire', *The Bath, Bristol, Tunbridge and Epsom Miscellany*, London, 1725, pp. 30—31.

36. Lewis Rouse, *Tunbridge Wells: or, a directory for the drinking of those waters*, London, 1725, p. 10. Rouse's work was originally published in 1632.

37. Robert Pierce, *The History and Memoirs of the Bath: containing Observations on what Cures have been there wrought, both by Bathing and Drinking those Waters*, London, 1713, p. 195.

38. *Scarborough Spaw or A Description of the Nature and Vertues of the Spaw at Scarbrough in Yorkshire*, York, 1667, p. 156.

39. See Jennifer Evans, *Aphrodisiacs, Fertility and Medicine in Early Modern England*, Boydell, Woodbridge, 2014, pp. 7—8.

40. 'A Song on the Multiplying Virtues of the Bath Waters. Humbly inscribed to the Citizen's Wives', in *The Bath, Bristol, Tunbridge and Epsom Miscellany. Containing Poems, Tales, Songs, Epigrams, Lampoons, Satires, Panegyricks, Amours, Intrigues, Etc.*, London, 1735, p. 5.

41. Quoted in Barbeau, *Life and Letters at Bath*, p. 9 n3.

42. Quoted by M. Jusserand, *A French Ambassador at the Court of Charles II: Le Comte de Cominge, from his unpublished correspondence*, T. Fisher Unwin, London, 1892, p. 217.

43. *A Philosophical and Medicinal Essay of the Waters of Tunbridge*, in *The Harleian Miscellany: a collection of scarce, curious and entertaining Pamphlets and Tracts*, vol. 1, London, 1808, pp. 587—8.

44. 'A Song: on the Multiplying Virtues of the Bath Waters. Humbly inscribed to the Citizen's Wives', in *The Bath, Bristol, Tunbridge and Epsom Miscellany*, London, 1725, pp. 11—13.

45. 'A Letter from Tunbridge to a Friend in London; being a Character of the Wells, and Company there', n.pag.

46. Thomas Shadwell, *Epsom-Wells, a Comedy. Acted at the Duke's Theatre*, London, 1673, p. 1, 1.1.

47. *John Wilmot, Earl of Rochester: Selected Poems*, ed. Paul Davis, Oxford University Press, Oxford, 2013, p. 69.

48. *The Scarborough Miscellany. An Original Collection of Poems, Odes, Tales, songs, Epigrams, etc. None which ever appear'd in Print before. By Several Hands*, London, 1732, p. 2.

49. Quoted in Ronald W. Cooley, '"Sexy in a 'Tunbridge Wells' Sort of Way": A Study in the Literary Iconography of Place', *Journal for Early Modern Cultural Studies* 15, Winter 2015, p. 105.

50. Eliza Haywood, *Baths — Intrigues in Four Letters to a Friend in London*, 3rd edn, London, 1725, p. 22.

51. Edward, Ward, *A Step to the Bath with a Character of the Place*, 2nd edn, London, 1700, p. 13.

52. Defoe, *The Fortunes and Misfortunes of the Famous Moll Flanders*, p. 106.

53. Baker, *Tunbridge-Walks*, p. 8.

54. Phyllis Hembry, *The English Spa 1560—1815: A Social History*, Athlone, London, 1990, p. 82.

55. Defoe, *A Tour thro' the Whole Island of Great Britain*, vol 2, p. 52.

56. *An Old Poem on the mineral wells at Islington, near London, describing the company who resorted to them*, ed. J.O. Halliwell, esq., F.R.S, London, 1861, reprinted from the poem entitled 'Islington Wells, or the Threepenny-Academy', London, 1691.

57. Ibid.

58. 'Lettres d'un Francois', 1745, quoted in Barbeau, *Life and Letters at Bath*, p. 82.

59. John Dunton, *Bumography: or, A Touch at The Lady's Tails, Being a Lampoon (Privately) Dispers'd at Tunbridge-Wells, in the Year 1707*, London, 1707, p. iii.

60. Baker, *Tunbridge-Walks*, p. 26.

61. *Eizabeth Montagu, the Queen of the Bluestockings*, vol. 2, ed. Emily J. Climenson, Cambridge University Press, Cambridge, 2011, p. 11.

62. Ibid.

63. *Mary Hamilton, afterwards Mrs John Dickenson, at court and at home: From letters and diaries, 1756 to 1816*, ed. Elizabeth and Florence Anson, J. Murray, London, 1925, p. 132.

SEVEN

1. Quoted in William Albert, *The Turnpike Road System in England: 1663–1840*, Cambridge University Press, Cambridge, 1972, p. 30.

2. Simeon Moreau, *A Tour to Cheltenham Spa; or, Gloucestershire display'd*, London, 1788, p. 206.

3. William Adam, *The Gem of the Peak; or, Matlock Bath and its Vicinity*, John & Charles Mosley, Derby, 1838, p. 36.

4. 'Scarborough Wells: A Satire', *The Bath, Bristol, Tunbridge and Epsom Miscellany*, London, 1725, pp. 30–31.

5. Quoted in David Hunter, *The Lives of George Frideric Handel*, Boydell, Woodbridge, 2015, p. 298.

6. *The Times*, 6 July 1785, p. 3.

7. Sir Thomas Elyot, *The Gouernour*, Everyman's Library, London, 1907, p. 75.

8. Richard Mulcaster, *Positions*, ed. Robert Hebert Quick, Longmans, Green, London, 1888, pp. 95–6.

9. Benjamin Franklin, *The Works of Benjamin Franklin*, Volume 1: *Autobiography, Letters and Misc. Writings 1725–1734*, ed. John Biglow, G.P. Putnam, New York, 1904, p. 100.

10. John Speed, 'A Commentary of Sea Water', in Richard Russell, *A Dissertation on the Use of Sea Water*, London, 1750, p. 154.

11. Ibid.

12. Quoted in Jeremy Black, *George III: America's Last King*, Yale University Press, New Haven CT and London, 2006, p. 383.

13. 'Cork' in *Pantologia: A New Cyclopaedia, Comprehending a Complete Series of Essays, Treatises, and Systems, Alphabetically Arranged*, vol. 3, C. Kearsley, London, 1813, n.pag.

14. Quoted in Fred Gray, *The Seaside: Architecture, Society and Nature*, Reaction Books, London, 2006, 147.

15. William Hutton, *A Description of Blackpool, in Lancashire; frequented for sea bathing*, Birmingham, 1789, p. 42.

16. See 'Piscator', *The Bath and the Beach; or, All about Bathing*, Sampson, Low, Marston, Low, and Searle, London, 1871, pp. 38–9.

17. Dr Speed, 'A Commentary on Sea Water', in Richard Russell, *A Dissertation on the Use of Sea Water*, London, 1750, pp. 149, 153.

18. Speed, 'A Commentary of Sea Water', p. vi.

19. Richard Russell, *A Dissertation on the use of Sea-Water in the Diseases of the Glands*, London, 1769, p. 72.

20. Thomas Pettigrew, ed., *Memoirs of the Life and Writings of the Late John Coakley Lettsom*, 3 vols, Longman, Hurst, Rees, Orme, & Brown, London, 1817, vol. 2, p. 156.

21. *Sea Bathing Infirmary at Margate open August 1, 1796*, London, 1798, p. 3.

22. Ibid., p. 8.

23. Pettigrew, ed., *Memoirs of the Life and Writings of the Late John Coakley Lettsom*, vol. 2, p. 157.

24. T.S. Eliot, 'The Waste Land', *The Criterion*, October 1922.

25. Gray, *The Seaside: Architecture, Society and Nature*, p. 178.

26. *The Lancet London: A Journal of British and Foreign Medicine, Surgery, Obstetrics, Physiology, Chemistry, Pharmacology, Public Health and News*, vol. 1, London, 1847, p. 450.

27. L.D.B., *Handbook of Droitwich and Its Neighbourhood: The Brine Baths and Salt Works*, Deighton & Son, Worcester, 1875, p. 23.
28. Ibid., pp. 24–5.
29. Ibid., p. 29.

EIGHT

1. 'The Founder of the Cold-Water Cure', *New England Journal of Medicine* 27, 1843 (Boston MA), p. 283.
2. Quoted in Virginia Smith, 'Gully, James Manby (1808–1883)', *Oxford Dictionary of National Biography*, Oxford University Press, Oxford, 2004; online edn, May 2014.
3. Ibid.
4. Quoted in Kathleen Denbigh, *A Hundred British Spas*, Spa Publications, Hong Kong, 1981, p. 175.
5. In 1757 Dr John Hall built a bathhouse at the Holy Well. At the end of the nineteenth century and up until the 1960s the Holy Well buildings were used as a commercial bottling plant for 'Malvern Seltzer'. St Ann's Well is high on the hill above Malvern Priory Church. In 1813 a well house was built over it in the style of a cottage. To reach it you either climbed the ninety-nine (today ninety-five) steps or rode up the hillside on a donkey. The Hay Well – now under the car park of the Baptist Church on Abbey Road – is the principal water source to the Hay Well Baths, which were built in 1834 by George Warwick. In 1842 Dr Gully took over the baths to treat his patients.
6. Dr John Wall, *Experiments and Observations on the Malvern Waters*, Worcester, 1757, p. 13.
7. Ibid., pp. 18–19.
8. Wells House was converted into a boys preparatory school in 1863, closing its doors in 1991. Today it has been converted into apartments.
9. Quoted in W.H. McMenemey, 'The Water Doctors of Malvern, with Special Reference to the Years 1842 to 1872', *Proceedings of the Royal Society of Medicine* 46, October 1952, p. 5.
10. Ibid., p. 6.
11. *The Correspondence of Charles Darwin*, Volume 4: *1847–1850*, ed. Frederick H. Burckhardt and Sydney Smith, Cambridge University Press, Cambridge, 1988, p. 225.
12. Joseph Leech, *Three Weeks in Wet Sheets; Being the Diary and Doings of a Moist Visitor to Malvern*, Hamilton, Adams, London, 1851, p. 2. Subsequent Leech quotations are taken from this edition.
13. Ibid., p. 9.
14. Ibid., p. 21.
15. According to Dr Wilson's handbook *The Water Cure* (1842) the dripping sheet is the first part of the water cure process and acts as a stimulant to the nervous and circulatory systems.
16. R.J. Raj et al., 'Effect of Cold Wet Sheet Pack on Body Temperature among Healthy Individuals: Result of a Single Arm Study', *Journal of Obesity and Overweight* 4, doi: 10.15744/2455-7633.4.101; Noreen Heer Nicol et al., 'Wet Wrap Therapy in Children with Moderate to Severe Atopic Dermatitis in a Multidisciplinary Treatment Program', *Journal of Allergy and Clinical Immunology* 2, 2014, pp. 400–406; Geetha B. Shetty et al., 'Effect of Naturopathic Treatment: Full Wet Sheet Pack on Autonomic Variables in Healthy Volunteers', *International Journal of Emerging Technologies and Innovative Research* 5, June 2018, pp. 171–6.
17. 'The Late Sir Francis Burdett', *The Times,* 27 January 1844, p. 5.
18. *The Times*, 20 June 1846, p. 7.

19. Richard Metcalfe, *The Rise and Progress of Hydrotherapy in England and Scotland*, Simkin, Marshall, Hamilton and Kent, London, 1912, p. 107.

20. Ibid., p. 200.

21. John Smedley, *Hydrotherapy and its Application to the Cure and Prevention of Diseases*, S.W. Partridge, London, 1861, p. xiv.

22. Quoted in Phyllis Hembry, *British Spas from 1815 to the Present*, Athlone, London, 1997, p. 177.

NINE

1. *The Times*, 29 September 1813, p. 4.

2. James Boswell, *The Life of Samuel Johnson, LL. D.: Including a Journal of a Tour to the Hebrides*, George Dearborn, New York, 1833, p. 265.

3. Michael La Beaume, *Observations on the Perspirator, or Portable Sudatory*, Simpkin & Marshall, London, 1846, p. v.

4. Ibid., p. 1.

5. *The Times*, 17 September 1821, p. 1.

6. *The Times*, 22 November 1848, p. 3.

7. *The Times*, 13 November 1847, p. 7.

8. Charles Whitlaw, 'On the Medicate Vegetable Vapour Bath', in Thomas Gill, *The Technical Repository*, T. Cadell, London, 1827, p. 123.

9. Charles Whitlaw, *The Scriptural Code of Health: With Observations on the Mosaic Prohibitions, and on the Principles and Benefits of the Medicated Vapour Bath*, London, 1838, p. 1.

10. Robert Culverwell, *The Life of Doctor Culverwell, Written by Himself*, London, 1855, p. 22.

11. *Sunday Times*, 23 April 1843, p. 1.

12. David Urquhart, *The Spirit of the East*, vol. 1, Henry Colburn, London, 1838, p. xxv.

13. Quoted in Malcolm Shifrin, 'The Victorian Turkish Bath: Its Origin, Development, & Gradual Decline', www.victorianturkishbath.org/2history/atozhist/ Hammam/3ClassSF.htm (accessed 10 October 2019).

14. David Urquhart, 'The Baths at Riverside', *The Free Press*, vol. 6, no. 17, 26 May 1858 (London), p. 130.

15. *Manchester Guardian*, 3 May 1858. p. 3.

16. See the reports in *The Times*, 8 July 1858, p. 6, and 9 July 1858, p. 12.

17. Quoted in Shifrin, 'The Victorian Turkish Bath'.

18. Quoted in ibid.

TEN

1. 'Manchester's Water Cure for Disabled Soldiers', *Manchester Guardian*, 10 February 1917.

2. Robert Fortescue Fox, 'The Future of British Spas', *Journal of the Royal Society of Arts*, vol. 65, no. 3351, 9 February 1917, pp. 218–28.

3. *The Spas of Britain: The Official Handbook of the British Spa Federation. For the Use of the Medical Profession*, Pitman Press, Bath, 1924, p. ix.

4. Quoted in Phyllis Hembry, *British Spas from 1815 to the Present*, Athlone, London, 1997, p. 243.

5. 'Opposition at Public Inquiry', *The Times*, 24 September 1954, p. 5.

6. 'Britain by the Sea: The Changing Pattern of Holidays', *The Times*, 11 September 1953, p. 5.

7. www.bathnes.gov.uk/services/your-council-and-democracy/local-research-and-statistics/wiki/tourism-and-visitor-economy (accessed September 2019).

Select Bibliography

Anon., *A Dream: or, The Force of Fancy. A Poem, containing characters of the Company now at the Bath*, Printed for Edmund Curll, London, 1710.

Anon., *A Rod for Tunbridge beaus, Bundl'd up at the Request of the Tunbridge Ladies, to Jirk Fools into more wit and clowns into more manners. A burlesque poem. To be published every summer, as long as the rakes continue their Rudeness, and the gentry their Vertue*, London, 1701.

Anon., *Bagatelle: or, the Bath Anniversary. A Poem*, 3rd edn, London, 1792.

Anon., *Characters at the Hot-Well, Bristol in September and at Bath in October, 1723*, London, 1724.

Anon., *The Bath, Bristol, Tunbridge and Epsom Miscellany*, London, 1725.

Anon., *The Diseases of Bath: A Satire unadorn'd with a Frontispiece*, London, 1737.

Anon., *The Foreigners Guide*, 4th edn, H. Kent, T. Hope, J. Joliffe and T. Pote, London, 1763.

Anon., 1682, from *The Blagford Ballards: Illustrating the Last years of the Stuarts*, pt III, ed. Joseph Woodall Ebsworth, Printed for the Ballad Society by S. Austin, Hertford, 1878.

Anon., *The New Bath Guide; or Useful pocket companion for all persons residing at or resorting to the ancient city*, Bath, 1784.

Anon., *The Register of Folly; or, Characters and Incidents at Bath and the Hot-wells, in a series of poetical epistles*, 4th edn, Bath, 1779.

Anon., *The Rival Beauties; A Poetical Contest*, Printed for W. Griffin, London, 1772.

Anon., *The Scarborough Miscellany. An Original Collection of Poems, Odes, Tales, songs, Epigrams, etc. None which ever appear'd in Print before. By Several Hands*, London, 1732.

Anon., *The Scarborough Miscellany: For the Year 1734 Being a Collection of Original Poems, Tales, Songs, Epigrams, Lampoons, Satires, and Panegyricks*, London, 1734.

Anon., *The Spas of Britain: The Official handbook of the British Spa Federation. For the use of the Medical Profession*, Pitman Press, Bath, 1924.

Anon., *The Tunbridge and Bath Miscellany for the Year 1714. Giving an exact description of those places, with characters of the Company*, London, 1714.

Anon., *Tunbrigialia; or, Tunbridge Miscellanies, For the Year 1719*, pt 1, 2nd edn, London, 1719.

Anon., *Tunbrigialia; or the Tunbridge Miscellany, for the Year 1722*, London, 1722.

Anon., *Tunbrigialia; or the Tunbridge Miscellany, for the Years 1737, 1738, 1739, being a curious collection of Miscellany poems and exhibited upon the walks at Tunbridge wells in the last three years. By a society of Gentlemen and Ladies*, London, 1739.

Ames, Richard, *An Old Poem on the mineral wells at Islington, near London, describing the company who resorted to them*, ed. J.O. Halliwell, esq., F.R.S., London, 1861; reprinted from poem entitled 'Islington Wells, or the Threepenny-Academy' by Richard Ames, Printed for E. Richardson, London, 1691.

Anderson, A.B., et al., *Vanishing Spas*, Friary Press, Dorchester, 1974.

Anstey, Christopher, *The New Bath Guide: or, Memoirs of the B—R—D Family in a series of Poetical Epistles*, London, 1766.

Arnold, Catherine, *City of Sin: London and Its Vices*, Simon & Schuster, London, 2010.

Baker, Thomas, *Tunbridge-Walks: or, the Yeoman of Kent*, Dublin, 1758.

Barbeau, A., *Life and Letters at Bath in the XVIIIth Century*, with a preface by Austin Dobson, William Heinemann, London, 1904.

Baylies, William, *Practical Reflections on the Uses and Abuses of Bath Waters*, London, 1757.

Benedict, Barbara, M., 'Consumptive Communities: Commodifying Nature in Spa Society', *The Eighteenth Century*, vol. 36, no. 3, Autumn 1995, 'The Contradictions of "Community"', pp. 203–19.

Berry, Sue, 'Pleasure Gardens in Georgian and Regency Seaside Resorts: Brighton, 1750–1840', *Garden History*, vol. 28, no. 2, Winter 2000, pp. 222–30

Bishop, Philippa, 'The Sentence of Momus: Satirical verse and Prints in Eighteenth-Century Bath', in *Bath History*, vol. V, Sutton Publishing, Stroud, 1994, pp. 51–79.

Bound, Reginald, ed., *Mrs Montagu, 'Queen of the Blues': Her letters and friendships from 1762 to 1800*, 2 vols, Constable, London, 1923.

Bradley, Ian C., *Water Music: Music Making in the Spas of Europe and North America*, Oxford University Press, Oxford, 2010.

Browne, Joseph, *Account of the Wonderful Cures performed by the Cold Baths*, Printed for J. How; and R. Borough and J. Baker, London, 1707.

Buchan, William, *Domestic Medicine, or a Treatise on the Prevention and cure of Diseases by Regimen and Simple Medicines*, J. Smith, London, 1830.

Chandler, Mary, *A Description of Bath: A Poem. Humbly inscribed to her Royal Highness the Princess Amelia*, London, 1734.

Cheyne, George, *An Account of the Nature and quality of bath-waters, the Manner of using them, and the Diseases in which they are proper*, London, 1738.

———*An Essay of the True Nature and due method of treating the gout, written for the use of Richard Tennison, Esq*, London, 1738.

Climenson, Emily J., ed., *Elizabeth Montagu, the Queen of the Bluestockings*, Cambridge University Press, Cambridge, 2011.

The Covent Garden Magazine Or the Amorous Repository, calculated Solely for the Entertainment of the Polite World and the Finishing of a Young Gentleman's Education IV, London, 1775.

Curl, James Stevens, 'Spas and Pleasure Gardens of London, from the Seventeenth to the Nineteenth Centuries', *Garden History*, vol. 7, no. 2, Summer 1979, pp. 27–68.

Davis, Graham, 'Entertainments in Georgian Bath: Gambling and Vice', in *Bath History*, vol. I, Sutton Publishing, Stroud, 1986, pp. 1–26.

Day, Martin, S., 'Anstey and Anapestic Satire in the late Eighteenth Century', *ELH*, vol. 15, no. 2, June 1948, pp. 122–46.

Deane, Edmund, *Spadacrene Anglica; or the English Spaw-Fountain*, John Grismand, London, 1626, ch. XI.

Defoe, Daniel, *A Tour thro' the Whole Island of Great Britain* [1724–27], vol. 1, 1724; vol. 2, 1725, Printed and sold by G. Strahan, London.

———*The Fortunes and Misfortunes of the Famous Moll Flanders*, ed. G.A. Starr, Oxford University Press, Oxford, 1998.

Essex, John, *The Dancing Master: or, The Art of Dancing Explained. Done from the French of Monsieur Rameau by J. Essex, Dancing Master*, London, 1728.

Falconer, Randle Wilbraham, *The Baths and Mineral Waters of Bath*, Royal College of Physicians of London, London, 1867.

Fawcett, Trevor, 'Chair Transport in Bath: The Sedan Era', in *Bath History*, vol. II, Sutton Publishing, Stroud, 1988, pp. 113–38.

———'Dance and Teachers of Dance in Eighteenth-Century Bath', in *Bath History*, vol. II, Sutton Publishing, Stroud, 1988, pp. 27–48.

———'Eighteenth-Century Shops and the Luxury Trade', in *Bath History*, vol. III, Sutton Publishing, Stroud, 1990, pp. 49–75.

———'Selling the Bath Waters: Medical Propaganda at an Eighteenth-Century Spa', *SANHS* 134, 1991, pp. 193–206.

———*Bath Entertain'd: Amusements, Recreations & Gambling at the Eighteenth Century Spa*, Rutton, Bath, 1998.

Fiennes, Celia, *The Illustrated Journeys of Celia Fiennes 1685–c. 1712*, ed. Christopher Morris, Short Run Press, Exeter, 2002.

Forde, Brownlow, *The Miraculous Cure: or, the Citizen Out-Witted. A Farce compiled by Brownlow Forde*, Newry, 1771.

Fox, Robert Fortescue, 'The Future of British Spas', *Journal of the Royal Society of Arts*, vol. 65, no. 3351, February 1917, pp. 218–28.

French, John, *The Yorkshire Spaw, or, a treatise of four famous medical wells, viz. the spas, or Vitrioline Well; the Stinking or Sulphur Well; the Dropping or Petrifying Well, and St. Mungo's Well near Knaresburgh in Yorkshire*, London, 1651.

Gale, Samuel, *A Tour Through Several Parts of England*, 1705, reprinted in John Nichols, *Antiquities in Lincolnshire: being the third volume of* the *Bibliotheca Topographica Britannica*, London, 1790.

Goldsmith, Oliver, *The Life of Beau Nash*, 2nd edn, London, 1762.

Graf, Holger Th., 'Sarah Scott: Female Historian in Mid-Eighteenth-Century Bath', in *Bath History*, vol. X, Sutton Publishing, Stroud, 2005, pp. 121–36.

Grainge, William, *The History and Topography of Harrogate, and the Forest of Knaresborough*, J.R. Smith, London, 1871.

Gray, Fred, *The Seaside: Architecture, Society and Nature*, Reaction Books, London, 2006.

Guidott, Thomas, *The Register of Bath*, London, 1694.

Haywood, Eliza, *Baths: Intrigues in Four Letters to a friend in London*, 3rd edn, London, 1725.

Heard, William, *The Snuff Box; Or, a Trip to Bath. A Comedy of Two Acts. By William Heard*, London, 1775.

Hembry, Phyllis, *The English Spa 1560–1815: A Social History*, Athlone, London, 1990.

———*British Spas from 1815 to the Present*, Athlone, London, 1997.

Herbert, Amanda E., 'Gender and the Spa: Space, Sociability and Self at British Health spas, 1640–1714', *Journal of Social History* 43, Winter 2009, pp. 361–82.

Hind, Thomas, *Tales from the Pump Room: Nine Hundred Years of Bath: The Place, its People and its Gossip*, Gollancz, London, 1988.

Hinderwell, Thomas, *The History and Antiquities of Scarborough*, 3rd edn, J. Bye, Scarborough, 1832.

Hurley, Alison E., 'A Conversation of Their own: Watering-Place Correspondence among the Bluestockings', *Eighteenth-Century Studies*, vol. 40, no. 1, Fall 2006, pp. 1–21.

Jones, Dr John, *The Bathes of Bathes Ayde*, London, 1572.

———*The Benefit of the Ancient Baths of Buckstones*, London, 1572.

Leech, Joseph, *Three Weeks in Wet Sheets; Being the diary and doings of A Moist Visitor to Malvern*, Hamilton, Adams, London, 1851.

Lucas, Charles, 'Of the City and thermal waters of Bath', in *An Essay on Waters*, vol. 3, London, 1756.

Macky, John, *A Journey Through England*, London, 1722.

Manco, Jean, 'The Cross Bath', in *Bath History*, vol. II, Sutton Publishing, Stroud, 1988, pp. 49–82.

McCormack, Kathleen, *George Elliot's English Travels: Composite Characters and Coded Communications*, Routledge, Abingdon, 2005.

Metcalf, Richard, *The Rise and Progress of Hydrotherapy in England and Scotland*, Simkin, Marshall, Hamilton and Kent, London, 1912.

Mitchell, Brigitte, 'English Spas', in *Bath History*, vol. I, Sutton Publishing, Stroud, 1986, pp. 189–204.

Neale, R.S., *Bath 1680–1850: A Social History or a Valley of Pleasure, Yet a Sink of Iniquity*, Routledge & Kegan Paul, London, 1981.

Nott, John, *Of the Hotwell Waters near Bristol*, 2nd edn, Bath and London,1797.

Odingsells, Gabriel, *Bath UnMask'd. A Comedy*, J. Walthoe, London, 1725.

O'Hare et al., Paper given at the Royal Society Symposium on the Bath Waters, London, 1987, quoted in Roger Rolls, 'Bath Cases: Care and Treatment of Patients at the Bath General Hospital during the Mid-Eighteenth Century', in *Bath History*, vol. II, Sutton Publishing, Stroud, 1988, p. 139–62.

Pepys, Samuel, *Memoirs of Samuel Pepys, Esq., F.R.S., Secretary to the Admiralty in the reigns of Charles II and James II: comprising his diary from 1659 to 1669*, ed. Richard Lord Braybrooke, 2nd edn, vol. IV, Henry Colburn, London, 1828.

Phippen, James, *Colbrans New Guide for Tunbridge Wells, being a Full and Accurate Description of the Wells and Its Neighbourhood within a Circuit of Nearly Twenty Miles, and Notices of the London and Dover Railway*, 2nd edn, J. Colbran, Tunbridge Wells, 1846.

Pierce, Robert, *The History and Memoirs of the Bath: containing Observations on what Cures have been there wrought, both by Bathing and Drinking those Waters*, London, 1713.

Priessnitz, Vincent, *The Cold Water Cure: Its Principles, Theory and Practice*, William Strange, London, 1843.

Rawlings, Thomas, *Tunbridge-Wells, or, A days courtship a comedy, as it is acted at the Dukes-Theatre. Written by a Person of Quality*, London, 1678.

Roberts, James, *The Diseases of Bath: A Satire, unadorn'd with a Frontispiece*, London, 1737.

Rogers. A.M., *Poems on various occasions, Consisting of original pieces, and translations, in two volumes*, Bath, 1783.

Rolls, Roger, 'Bath Cases: Care and Treatment of Patients at the Bath General Hospital during the Mid-Eighteenth Century', in *Bath History*, vol. II, Sutton Publishing, Stroud, 1988, pp. 139–62.

Rotherham, Ian D., *Spas and Spa Visiting*, Shire Publications, Oxford, 2014.

Rouse, Lewis, *Tunbridge Wells: or, a directory for the drinking of those waters*, London, 1725.

Russell, Richard, *A Dissertation on the use of Sea-Water in the Diseases of the the Glands*, 4th edn, London, 1760.

Ryder, Dudley, *The Diary of Dudley Ryder 1715–1716*, Transcribed by shorthand and edited by William Matthews, Methuen, London, 1939.

Shadwell, Thomas, *Epsom-Wells, a Comedy. Acted at the Duke's Theatre*, London, 1673.

Sheridan, Richard Brinsley, *The Rivals: A Comedy. As Acted at the Theatre-Royal in Covent-Garden*, 2nd edn, Printed for John Wilkie, London, 1775.

Short, Thomas, *An Essay towards a Natural, Experimental, and Medicinal History of the principle Mineral Waters of Cumberland, Northumberland, Westmoreland...*, Sheffield, 1740.

Smedley, John, *Hydrotherapy and Its Application to the Cure and Prevention of Diseases*, S.W. Partridge, London, 1861.

Smith Surtees, Robert, *Handley Cross; or, Mr. Jorrock's Hunt*, with illustrations by John Leech, Bradbury, Agnew & Co., London, 1854.

Smollett, Tobias, *The Adventures of Peregrine Pickle, in which are included Memoirs of a Lady of Quality*, vol. II (1751), George Routledge and Sons, London, 1882.

———*An Essay on the External Use of water in a letter to Dr. — With Particular remarks upon the present method of using the Mineral waters at Bath in Somersetshire, and a plan for rendering them more safe, agreeable, and efficacious*, M. Cooper, London, 1752.

———*The Expedition of Humphrey Clinker*, 1771, ed. Peter Miles, Everyman, London, 1993.

Sprange, J., *The Tunbridge Wells Guide, or an Account of the Ancient and Present State of that Place, to which is Added a Particular Description of the Towns and Villages, ... within the Circumference of Sixteen Miles*, Tunbridge Wells, 1780.

Thicknesse, Philip, *The New Prose Bath Guide for the Year 1778*, London, 1778.

———*The Valetudinarians Bath Guide. Or, the Means of Obtaining Long Life and Health*, London, 1780.

Thornbury, Walter, 'Coldbath Fields and Spa Fields', in *Old and New London*, vol. 2, Cassell, Petter & Galpin, London, 1878.

The Tradesman's and Traveller's Pocket Companion: or, the Bath and Bristol Guide: calculated for the Use of Gentlemen and Ladies who visit Bath; The inhabitants of Bath and Bristol; All persons who have occasion to Travel, 2nd edn, Thomas Boddely, Bath, 1753.

Turner, Dr William, *A Book of the Natures and Properties as well of the Baths in England as of other baths in Germany and Italy*, Arnold Birckman, Cologne, 1568.

Wall, Dr John, *Experiments and Observations on the Malvern waters*, Worcester, 1757.

Ward, Edward, *A Step to the Bath with a Character of the Place*, 2nd edn, London, 1700.

Weber, Herman, et al., *The Mineral Waters and Health Resorts of Europe*, Smith, Elder & Co., London, 1898.

Wilson, Ellen, 'A Shropshire Lady in Bath 1794–1807', in *Bath History*, vol. IV, Sutton Publishing, Stroud, 1992, pp. 95–123.

Woolley, Hannah, *The Gentlewoman's Companion; or A Guide to the Female Sex*, London, 1675.

Wroughton, John, '"At the Gates of Hell": The Seamy Side of Life in Seventeenth-Century Bath', *Bath History*, vol. X, Sutton Publishing, Stroud, 2005, pp. 28–47.

Picture Credits

Index